THE INTEREST-BASED BASED LEARNING COACH

THE INTEREST-BASED BASED

LEARNING COACH

A Step-by-Step Playbook for Genius Hour, Passion Projects, and Makerspaces in School

Jeanne H. Purcell, Ph.D., Deborah E. Burns, Ph.D., & Wellesley H. Purcell

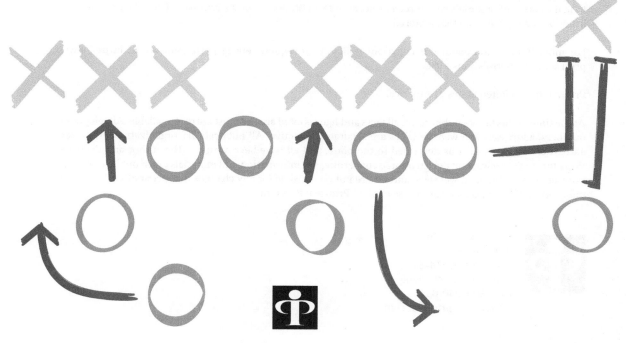

PRUFROCK PRESS INC.
WACO, TEXAS

Prufrock Press Inc.
P.O. Box 8813
Waco, TX 76714-8813
Phone: (800) 998-2208
Fax: (800) 240-0333
http://www.prufrock.com

TABLE OF CONTENTS

FOREWORD

AS I was completing my 20th year as a middle school teacher, I was also writing my dissertation and, although I did not know it at the time, getting ready to begin a "second life" as a university faculty member. The dissertation centered around the way two middle school teachers made sense of the fraternal twin concepts of curriculum and instruction. The time I spent observing and talking with them made my dissertation a labor of love rather than a benchmark to be checked off on a list of graduation requirements. That experience also solidified my sense of what makes some teachers life-changers and, in that way, provided a much-needed compass for my early university teaching in the areas of curriculum and instruction.

Judy Schlim and Dianne Weigel were teachers in the small town where I worked for 2 decades, and where I learned about life, myself, and the fine art of teaching. Similar in some ways, they were quite different in other ways. They were both in their 40s, parents of adolescents, and fueled by a passion for teaching youth. Judy was a veteran teacher—probably at about the 20-year mark, as I was. Dianne, who was about the same age, was a new teacher. Having opted to be at home as much as possible while her own children grew up, she was beginning her career as a public school educator when I met her 2 years before I began work on my dissertation. Both teachers were student-focused, and both were quite reflective about their own work. What I knew of their work gave me confidence that time I spent in their classrooms would be time well spent. It was much more instructive and inspiring than I could have imagined.

I replay scenarios from their classrooms often, even though more than 2 decades have passed since they allowed me to enter their worlds. Two images from their classrooms seem useful in framing this book.

Dianne's students seemed always to be wholly comfortable with her—sometimes almost reverent. She was a master at leading discussions based on literature she and her students shared. The questions she asked were invitations for her students to consider life in ways that were both unfamiliar and invitational to them. One thing she did that caught me off-guard every time was standing in front of the room to launch a discussion, then disappearing into a student seat once the students began sharing ideas. She gave the kids the reins of the conversation and sat, almost invisible, among them—listening intently to their ideas and studying their responses. The students addressed one another and routinely kept conversations going for half an hour or more without any need for teacher direction. It was a lovely thing to see.

Because the content was new to her, however, occasionally, when she was explaining an idea to them, she would make an error. That was the case on a day when she taught point of view in literature, treating the concept as though it were a synonym for viewpoint. I wondered if some of the students caught the error, but then realized as they discussed a story they had just completed that they had not only caught the error, but self-corrected and were using the term as it is typically used in talking about the architecture of a piece of fiction.

When I interviewed Dianne's middle school students, it was evident that they greatly valued her role in their young lives, and I took a chance at one point to ask a student if he ever noticed when she presented an idea or concept in a way that was a little "off" in comparison to their prior understanding. He looked at me curiously and said, "Well, of course we see that happen sometimes, but it's not important. We figure it out." He paused briefly and continued, "See, here's the thing, all of our other teachers told us what to think and what to learn. She has taught us how to think and how to learn. That's way more important than a definition we can look up if we need to."

Dianne's students found her approach to teaching to be interesting, relevant, and even electric because she gave them structure, trust, and freedom to use their minds.

Judy's approach to teaching history to her middle school students was, in key ways, like Dianne's, in her trust that the young learners could make meaning from content, not just repeat it. In interviews, many of her students said to me, "You know, in our class, we hate the history textbook!" Attempting to be a good interviewer, I'd say, "Really? Tell me more about that. How does it work?" Their response was always something like, "Oh, well we read the book before we start our study of a topic so we can lay a foundation, but then we leave the book alone and learn the real history."

Judy's years in the classroom had been a continuing exercise in creative planning. She seemed to have a bottomless well of explorations, challenges, and real-world products through which her students could see the complexity and value of probing the past and connecting it with the present.

One day as she was about to invite her students to join her in seeing the Civil War through multiple lenses, she told them it was always her favorite unit because it could teach them so much about themselves, their country, people's inevitable short-sightedness, and their ability to learn from their mistakes, if they had the courage to do that. She told them several things they would be doing to help them think deeply about that time period and its impact on the U.S. today. The students' faces reflected anticipation. Then she asked an off-the-cuff question. "Are you as excited as I am about studying the Civil War?" Their faces squinted and drooped—and clearly, they were not answering in the affirmative.

She paused for a moment, thinking, and said, "Well, maybe it's not that I care so much that you're as excited as I am about studying the Civil War. Maybe what I really care about is that there is something you'd get excited to learn about if you had the chance."

Still adapting her thinking as she went, she asked the students to tell her topics they would be happy to spend time learning about at night and on weekends. They provided a long list, which she recorded on the board—sports, games, food, teenagers, music, medicine, families, clothing, politics, heroes, villains, books . . .

She gave each student an index card and asked them to put their name on the top line, write the numerals 1, 2, and 3 down the side of the card, and then list three topics they'd be eager to learn about if they had the opportunity, with number one as their first choice, two as second choice, and so on.

When she returned to class the next day, she returned the cards to their owners, noting that she had circled one of the items on each person's card—choosing number 1 any time that was feasible. She told the students they would be doing a "sidebar study." "I'll go home every night to develop questions, experiences, and conversations we can have that will help us think about why the Civil War time period is so important in our past history and in our present. Your job is to go home every night and study the topic I circled on your list. The only requirement is that you study the topic as it existed during the Civil War—so music during the Civil War, games during the Civil War, clothing during the Civil War, and so on."

And that is how the unit unfolded. Every day, students waved their hands with energy that was hard to contain as they shared how their topics connected to the day's focus. The synergy was electric. Every kid "owned" the unit, and they owned it together as well.

When Judy asked the students to critique the unit, as she always did as they concluded a study, a great majority of students wrote that this was the most important piece of history they had ever studied because it taught them so much about themselves individually and about how events in one time period continue to shape later times.

Both Dianne's and Judy's teaching were, day after day, dynamic and invitational. Both teachers strived to make their content interesting and relevant to students so that they could make meaning of what they were learning and connect it to their own experiences. Judy was especially skilled at also building on students' personal interests.

There is a difference between those two instructional approaches. Interesting learning opportunities capture students' attention and imagination—often helping them discover new interests. Making purposeful opportunities for students to explore their own personal interests adds another dimension of depth and appeal to learning. Both interesting instruction and interest-based instruction are hallmarks of quality teaching.

The authors of this book have used their combined and considerable experience as teachers and leaders of teachers to provide guidelines and highly practical tools for creating learning experiences that are interesting to young learners—therefore engaging their minds—and that can be interest-based—therefore giving them opportunity to develop their particular skills, talents, and passions. The explanations and illustrations provided in the book make a clear case that interest-based learning shouldn't be something apart from quality instruction, but that it, in fact, draws on our best understanding of meaningful content and high-yield assessment practices, while also mentoring student development of the habits of mind and work that result in agency as learners. Equally important, learning to design and guide instruction that commends learning to young people draws on teachers' creativity and extends their agency as well. Good news all around for today's classrooms.

—Carol Ann Tomlinson
Author of *How to Differentiate Instruction in
Academically Diverse Classrooms* (3rd ed.)

INTRODUCTION

WELCOME! We are delighted that you have chosen this book and that the topic of interest-based learning intrigues you. We hope the text's content, strategies, and resources meet your expectations, address your needs, and support your continued commitment to students' self-designed questions and explorations.

This introduction:

1. provides an explanation of the book's focus,
2. explains the book's purpose,
3. describes the various types of educators who might find the text's content and strategies useful,
4. reviews the book's goals for teachers and students,
5. explains the book's organizational structure, and
6. shares a brief description of the content and sequence of each chapter.

What Is the Focus of This Book?

This is a book about interest-based learning (IBL): what it is, why it matters, and how to address different students' interests within a standards-based learning environment. This practical book walks through an eight-step interest-based learning process and explains how it can be implemented within the general education curriculum during a short time allocation on a weekly or twice-weekly basis. The book is full of examples, case studies and related recommendations, timelines, options, templates, planning and communication tools, and assessment, feedback, and evaluation strategies.

Although a one-on-one learning experience might be perceived as the ideal learning situation, teachers rarely have that luxury. Instead, this book posits IBL within the parameters of a classroom in which one teacher has the responsibility of teaching numerous subject areas to one class of students or one subject area to several classes. We honor the importance of a high-quality, standards-based curriculum that is coupled with personalization and differentiation based on students' individual interests and questions. This text explains the philosophy that guides the IBL framework and related research about the impact of IBL on students' skills, attitudes, understandings, and dispositions, but our emphasis is on planning, methods, and actions.

The text is designed to support your understanding of IBL, explore the options for implementing it in your own school and classroom settings, and, most importantly, provide strategies for you to design your own system that addresses your students' characteristics and school expectations.

Why Did We Write This Book?

As you've probably already noticed, three authors worked collaboratively to write this text. We made the decision to work together because all three of us, regardless of our varied experiences, have a strong commitment to and belief in the power of student-centered learning and student interests. Our attachment to IBL stems from our numerous experiences as children, students, classroom teachers, program specialists, administrators, and university faculty. You have likely had similar professional responsibilities and opportunities for engaging, choice-based experiences.

During the early years of our preservice and inservice training, as well as our graduate education courses, our professors, supervisors, and mentors continually emphasized the importance of a nurturing classroom environment and the need to offer experiences that recognize and address the individual learning needs and strengths of our students. Back in those dark ages, individualized learning was emphasized as best practice. Later in our careers, we become more deeply involved in both differentiation and interest-based gifted education. They were natural bridges to our earlier adventures with individualized education and community building.

Like many of you, we have been fortunate to have many different kinds of opportunities, both as children and as adults, that have allowed us to experience the joys and intense captivation that often accompany our involvement in tailor-made, interest-based projects, both as adults and when we were children. We have also enjoyed the delightful curiosity and unending questions of preschoolers and witnessed the power of interest in supporting engagement, self-determination, persistence, and student agency. These are life skills and dispositions, not just school-related frames of mind, and we believe that they should be nurtured in all children. Our experiences have led to our commitment to retaining and fortifying such curiosity and inquiry beyond preschool, throughout students' school careers, and during the whole of their adult lives. We hope you feel the same way.

Our purposes for this text are fourfold. First, and foremost, we aim to win you over and to support your work as advocates for interest-based inquiry. Accordingly, we share a strong rationale for making room for individual student interests and inquiry. Second, we attempt to clarify the similarities among the numerous, current models for interest-based learning to eliminate the need to choose among them (e.g., Genius Hour, passion projects, Makerspaces, or project- and problem-based learning). Instead, we focus on an eight-step process that is universal to all IBL options and on the more practical implementation and management issues related to IBL, regardless of the model selected. We also provide methods for making time for interest-based inquiry within a crowded curriculum. Several IBL models specify 20% of classroom time. We would be delighted if all readers were able to carve out this much time! As realists, we settle for designating a small and reasonable portion of classroom time.

Third, we offer a flexible structure and calendar for initiating and organizing such projects and tasks. This third purpose best aligns with the "playbook" concept in the book's title. Just as a football playbook describes the various ways that a football team might organize itself to move the ball down the field, this book details the process for moving students' interests "down the field," culminating in interest-based learning and sometimes product development and sharing. Fourth, and last, we discuss suggestions and processes for sharing student work and for evaluating student learning and growth. We found little guidance regarding these last two processes as we conducted background reading for this guidebook.

Who Might Find This Book Useful?

This book was written for teachers who are curious about interest-based learning. The text is also designed for those who are interested in practical strategies for managing each phase of the IBL process. This is not a book for educators who want to focus their entire curriculum on student interests, nor is it a book for teachers who are firmly committed to identical learning experiences for all learners.

In some cases, teachers may have heard about IBL and agree with its goals and purposes. These readers are looking for more in-depth information and practical suggestions. Other readers are likely to have experimented with IBL and are searching for others' perspectives about management and organization. Having said that, our experiences convince us that, in addition to classroom and subject-area teachers, many school librarians, club leaders, and technology and gifted education specialists also see the benefits of interest-based learning options. These colleagues are impelled to add interest-based offerings to a portion of their curriculum, often for the expressed purpose of emphasizing student strengths, supporting the real-world application of academic concepts, and promoting engagement and talent development. To that end, we often present ideas for implementing IBL models in alternative settings.

In addition to these specialists, school and district administrators and graduate education faculty and candidates may also find this text useful as they analyze and evaluate the various curriculum models and teaching strategies available for instructional design. For these reasons, Chapter 1 not only addresses the concepts and guiding principles related to IBL, but also provides a comparison between the interest-based learning framework and other curriculum models, such as Genius Hour, passion projects, Makerspaces, project-based learning, expeditionary learning, and problem-based learning.

What Are the Goals for Each Chapter?

There are specific goals that direct the writing and organization of this book. Chapter 1 describes and provides examples of IBL. It includes a comparison and contrast of the concept of interest-based learning (as it is represented in this text) with other teaching and learning frameworks that foster inquiry, student self-direction, and planning (e.g., Genius Hour, passion projects, Makerspaces, problem-based learning, or project-based learning). Chapter 2 identifies and describes the preparatory tasks that need to be planned and organized before teachers and students begin any IBL opportunities. Chapter 3 provides strategies for creating a shared classroom vision for IBL.

Chapter 4 provides a rationale for addressing assessment as one of the first decision-making and planning tasks for any teacher who has made a commitment to IBL. The chapter reviews the purpose, structure, and options for interest-based learning goals and formative assessment. The bulk of the chapter focuses on formative assessment strategies and tools for student-teacher goal setting and assessment criteria, class record-keeping, status checks, conferences, formative assessment, evidence gathering options, student self-evaluation, and feedback. Chapter 5 features tools and techniques for determining individual student interests.

Chapter 6 offers tools and processes for focusing students' interests into manageable and researchable inquiry questions or goal statements. Chapter 7 includes methods, templates, and resources for the organization, implementation, management, and coaching of students' IBL projects. Resources are the engine that supports students' interest-based learning, and Chapter 8 offers tactics for identifying, locating, judging the worthiness of, and managing students' research resources. Chapter 9 is devoted to the researching, investigating, exploring, experimenting, and designing that students will conduct about their targeted inquiry question. As such, it comprises the bulk of students' time in an IBL initiative.

Products need to be well-aligned with students' inquiry questions and goals. Chapter 10 provides strategies and tools for selecting appropriate student inquiry products, should they be pursued. Chapter 11 helps educators and students select appropriate and manageable audiences, beyond the classroom teacher, for student research. Chapter 12, the final chapter, provides reflective questions that can be used to assess the overall effectiveness of the IBL initiative, as well as suggestions for celebrating successes along the way.

In addition to these specific chapter goals, we also have two additional goals for the text as a whole. First, we hope to enhance your self-efficacy for coaching and supporting IBL in your classroom through the provision of customizable templates. Second, we aim to illustrate how IBL could be implemented in settings other than the general classroom.

How Is Each Chapter Organized?

To support your understanding, each chapter contains 10 common elements. At the beginning of each chapter, you will find (1) a quotation that captures the essence of the chapter's content. This is followed by (2) a list of the goals that will be covered in each chapter. You may find it helpful to use these guiding goals to support and check your understanding. These goals can also be used to tailor your interests to specific segments within each chapter.

The goals and guiding questions are followed by information prefaced with the appropriate guiding question. Examples are also included, when relevant. These examples may be written as (3) direct quotations from students or (4) case studies. The quotations and reflections create opportunities for your linkages, shifts, and site-based modifications. The case studies were gleaned from various grade levels and subject areas. They focus on realistic implementation issues with interest-based learning, as experienced by teachers and students who have been given fictitious names. Two case studies, Andrea and Pablo, are threaded through the chapters to illustrate how the two students' projects morph throughout each stage of the process. An additional six case studies are included in Appendix A. Each was purposefully selected to highlight a common challenge faced by practitioners in the IBL implementation process. Teacher-generated solutions are shared in each of the six case studies included in Appendix A.

When appropriate, the text also includes (5) suggestions for divergent school situations (e.g., amount of school time available, the middle school context, a school library setting, behavior management issues). They come from our collective field experiences. In addition, (6) tables, (7) figures, and (8) reproducible resources provide illustrations, design options, and more in-depth information.

Editable templates of many of the reproducible resources are available on the book's webpage at https://www.prufrock.com/Interest-Based-Learning-Coach-Resources. aspx. The templates will make your work efficient and support customization.

There is also (9) a list of references that detail the sources used in the development of each chapter. These references are also intended as additional resources if you want to delve further into the content. Finally, a (10) conclusion or summary, aligned to the chapter goals, ends each chapter and provides a reminder of the learning that occurred. Lastly, although we are unable to engage in a true dialogue with you, we have chosen to use a conversational tone throughout this text.

How Is the Text Sequenced?

This text is organized around the IBL framework that is illustrated in Figure 1. The pedestal, at the bottom of the figure, shows that a strong foundation is critical to the success of any IBL initiative. The foundation consists of several prerequisites explained in detail in Chapter 2. The foundation must also include a clear vision for the process that is shared by all key stakeholders. A shared vision is such an important prerequisite that we devote Chapter 3 to this cornerstone.

Moving up the figure, you will see three circles, or rings, nested inside each other. As with a Venn diagram, the rings showcase the relationships among the

FIGURE 1
Interest-Based Learning Coaching Framework

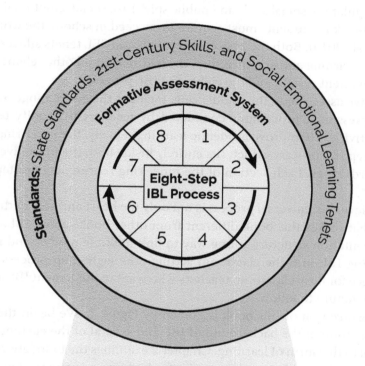

Foundational Elements

Establishing Prerequisites | **Creating a Shared Vision**

Eight-Step IBL Process

Step 1: Finding Interests
Step 2: Focusing Interests
Step 3: Goal Setting, Developing Inquiry Questions, and Mapping Plans
Step 4: Finding and Managing Resources
Step 5: Researching, Investigating, Exploring, Experimenting, and Designing
Step 6: Determining and Designing Products
Step 7: Tapping Potential Audiences
Step 8: Reflecting, Debriefing, and Celebrating

fundamentals of IBL. The outer ring represents state standards, 21st-century skills (Partnership for 21st Century Learning [P21], 2019), and tenets of social-emotional learning (SEL). The five tenets of SEL (identity and agency, emotional regulation, cognitive regulation, social skills and public spirit) are social, emotional, behavioral, and character skills students must acquire to succeed in school, the workplace, and life (Frey et al., 2019). Both the 21st-century skills and SEL tenets affect every aspect of academic learning and are, therefore, the bedrock for all other elements: the formative assessment system and the eight-step IBL process.

Formative assessment, the middle ring, includes the entire range of formal and informal assessment procedures conducted by teachers to modify teaching and learning activities to improve academic learning. Finally, the inner ring represents the eight-step IBL process, which sits entirely inside both the formative assessment and standards rings. Each section of the inner ring represents one step in the IBL process.

We believe this universal process is not only the heart and soul of this playbook, but also what makes this book different from other books about IBL. The universal implementation structure is one way to link multiple models and methods for incorporating IBL into the classroom setting. The eight-step process may be the missing piece for busy classroom teachers who want to implement IBL and have not yet had a structure to follow.

The organization of this book is guided by Figure 1. We begin the text with a brief examination of the background of IBL and several of the current models and approaches to this form of learning. Chapter 2 examines the foundational elements, and Chapter 3 shares ideas and strategies for building a common shared vision for an IBL initiative. Beyond these introductory sections, the text proceeds through the eight-step process.

The only exception is the chapter on formative assessments. We have chosen to place this important topic in Chapter 4, following the backward design tenets of Wiggins and McTighe (1998) and because it is such a central tenet of IBL. With assessment always in the forefront, you will be aware of your primary goal in an IBL initiative: moving students closer to their goals.

CHAPTER 1

Interest-Based Learning and Its Counterparts

> If one has failed to develop curiosity and interest in the early years, it is a good idea to acquire them now, before it is too late to improve the quality of life. . . . There are literally millions of potentially interesting things in the world to see, to do, to learn about. But they do not become actually interesting until we devote attention to them.
>
> —Mihaly Csikszentmihalyi, *Finding Flow*

Genius Hour, passion projects, Makerspaces, and problem- and project-based learning are wonderful opportunities for students to find, explore, study, problem solve, and create with their interests. This book provides a supporting framework for organizing and coaching the interest-based learning process with students who may have little experience designing their own learning paths.

This chapter reviews the IBL process and the steps and strategies students and teachers can use to organize their work. Specifically, we explain the framework, components, and overarching expectations and connections illustrated in Figure 1 (p. 7). In addition, we have included an explanation of the goals for IBL, its rationale, and a short review of related research. The last section compares interest-based learning models such as Genius Hour, passion projects, Makerspaces, and the more generic project-based and problem-based models. Lastly, we clarify how the IBL framework can be used to support teachers' and students' work within the context of each of the other models.

As a result of reading, reasoning with, and discussing the content in Chapter 1, you will be able to:

1. define and give examples of interest-based learning;
2. provide a rationale for including interest-based learning within the curriculum;
3. link academic, literacy, 21st-century, and social-emotional learning standards with the goals and process for learning;
4. describe the framework, components, and process that support interest-based learning;
5. explain the research related to interest-based learning; and
6. compare the framework in this book with current inquiry learning models.

What Is Interest-Based Learning?

When you hear the phrase "interest-based learning in the classroom," what do you imagine? Pure pandemonium? Students shooting hoops, playing video games, and updating their social media accounts? Not so fast. Sure, sports, technology, and friendship are popular student interests, but we're talking about interest-based learning in this text, and the three previously mentioned activities fall more into the "activity" department than they do into the learning category. On the other hand, if you've helped a student expand their interest in video games by suggesting that they learn how to code so that they could design their own games, then that is a solid example of IBL and coaching.

Merriam-Webster defines *interest* as "a feeling of wanting to learn more about something or to be involved in something." The definition continues: "Interest is a quality that attracts a person's attention and makes them want to learn more about something or to be involved in something." In this text, we append the word *learning* to the term *interest* in order to clarify the purpose for the inclusion of interests within curriculum and to amplify the meaning of interests beyond mere enjoyment. In a complementary fashion, IBL employs students' interests as the gateway for the development of students' project goals, learning questions, engagement, and self-management.

This book advocates for a designated time of the week or corner in the curriculum that allows for choice and encourages students to ask and answer their own IBL questions and to develop their own explorations, design projects, and development goals. As such, when they are tied to learning—the chief purpose for education and schooling—interests become a rightful and deserving part of the curriculum. In order to support learning and engagement, IBL projects always begin with the identification of students' interests (see Chapter 5).

Interest identification is followed by the development of a focused goal or question that guides the design, experimentation, tinkering, construction, research, and problem solving inherent in such projects (see Chapter 6). The attention to goals and questions helps students frame the purpose for their projects and identify the formal or informal learning that must take place to achieve the goals and answer the questions. The journey from students' known to unknown knowledge, skills, and applications ensures that each project truly illustrates new learning and not merely a repetition of previous actions and understandings.

Examples of IBL might include:

× a kindergarten student who wants to learn how to use the various shapes of the wooden classroom blocks to create a replica of the Tappan Zee Bridge in New York;

× a sixth-grade student who becomes fascinated by the estuary display in San Francisco's Exploratorium museum and volunteers to collect and test water samples in nearby Oakland, CA;

× an eighth-grade student who learns about food insecurity in social studies class and works with some classmates to educate others and raise money for a local food bank;

× a second-grade student who wants to write letters to famous people to see if they will write back; or

× a fifth-grade student who wants to learn about architecture and blueprints in order to design a home.

Why Include IBL Within the Curriculum?

There are many reasons to include interest-based learning in a classroom, grade-level, or school curriculum. Some of these motives address students' intrapersonal skills, mindsets, and dispositions. Others are academic and social traits.

Student agency, a facet of intrapersonal intelligence, is the primary reason most educators choose to become involved in interest-based learning, especially when they sense issues regarding students' passive compliance or disengagement. Building student agency means providing opportunities for students to direct their own learning, using goals, tasks, and resources that are personally interesting and relevant, thereby encouraging self-initiation.

If the essentials are in place, and the shared vision credible (see Chapters 2 and 3, respectively), then additional intrapersonal dispositions and skills are likely to grow as well. These include authentic engagement and the development of students' self-management skills, self-efficacy, curiosity, growth mindset, and intrinsic motivation for learning. Depending on the nature of each project, students will also have the opportunity to enhance their reasoning skills, including, but not limited to, analytic thinking, planning, decision making, organization, problem solving, creativity, research, and communication. Teacher-student conferences that ask students to discuss and reflect on these attitudes and skills also support students' self-awareness, self-evaluation, and related goal setting.

Second, the rationale for IBL also includes opportunities to strengthen academic standards. Projects always involve some type of content and, as such, offer students opportunities to learn, deepen, or apply their understanding of core concepts, skills, and principles in the academic area most related to their interest. For example, the sixth-grade student who collected and studied water samples also learned and applied Next Generation Science Standards (NGSS Lead States, 2013) related to precision, identification, and measurement. He also deepened and applied his understanding of NGSS Disciplinary Core Ideas, such as salinity, pollution, habitat, and ecosystem interactions.

In addition to content knowledge and skill standards, social-emotional learning standards are also inherent in IBL projects. Reading, writing, listening, speaking, research, self-management, reasoning, organization, and collaboration skills are integral to students' inquiries, although any specific standard's linkage is unique to students' individual projects. The expectation that students learn and apply these skills makes them relevant and necessary in the immediate moment and more likely to be linked to the success of students' work.

Third, the rationale for IBL also includes the opportunity to develop students' social skills and dispositions. Individual, partner, and small-group projects provide natural opportunities that allow educators to teach and coach traits and skills such as empathy, collaboration, active listening, relationship building, and an appreciation for the perspective of others. The classroom culture benefits from students sharing and celebrating the interests, goals, and accomplishments of others.

"So," you ask, "are there any reasons not to implement IBL?" There are. Concerns related to parental, administrative, and collegial support; time constraints; the need for varied resources; classroom space; the multitasking required to manage numerous projects among individuals and small groups of students; and students' levels of self-management all weigh on teachers' minds as they decide whether or not IBL is relevant and doable in their situation. Chapters 2 and 3 suggest how to address these concerns, so make a quick list of any issues that you have, keep an open mind, and reconsider your perspective at the end of Chapter 3.

How Are Academic, Social-Emotional, and 21st-Century Learning Goals Linked to IBL?

IBL is grounded in students' interests. These interests are wide-ranging and specific to each child. Interests serve as the motivation for students' effort and persistence during the course of their projects. But how are these real-world interests aligned to the academic, 21st-century, and social-emotional learning standards that govern curriculum? After all, these standards are one of educators' first priorities.

Start with a closer look at the language arts standards specified for each grade level and subject area. How are they aligned with IBL projects? Whether you are considering the Common Core State Standards for English Language Arts (CCSS-ELA) or individual states' language arts and content literacy standards, most educators would agree that the standards' emphasis on reading, writing, research, speaking, and listening skills are naturally linked to the work students do during the course of IBL projects. Students read about their interest area, they conduct research and take notes, and they critically evaluate the topic-specific writings of other people who specialize in their interest area. Often, students also do their own topic-based writing, speaking, and listening. All of these actions foster deeper learning and an application of these literacy standards to each IBL project.

But what about science, social studies, and math standards? Are they also aligned with student learning during the IBL process? The CCSS math practices, with their attention to problem solving, precision, abstract reasoning, argumentation, and the use of tools and structures, are well-aligned with the nature of an inquiry project (National Governors Association Center for Best Practices [NGA] & Council of Chief State School Officers [CCSSO], 2010b). However, the specific math standards related to numeration, algebra, geometry, etc., coordinate only with the work of those students engaged in a math project that applies such skills. In a similar manner, if a student is investigating a science interest, there may or may not be an alignment with the NGSS, depending on the topic and its NGSS grade level placement. The same is true for the social studies standards (National Council for the Social Studies [NCSS], 2013). Their inquiry, research, informative and argument writing, and listening and speaking expectations align well with most social studies IBL projects. Again, the alignment to a specific topic standard in social studies depends on the nature of students' individual projects and the grade level placement of a standard.

Finally, consider the alignment of the tenets of social-emotional learning (Frey et al., 2019) and 21st-century skills (P21, 2019). Can these standards be learned, practiced, or applied over the course of an IBL project? Our emphatic answer is

"Yes!" The SEL tenets address intrapersonal and social skills, dispositions, and attitudes, such as agency, collaboration, and self-management. The 21st-century skills focus on reasoning skills, such as problem solving, design, planning, and decision making. These traits are inherent in nearly all IBL projects.

"Independent research contributes to my growth as a student more so than any other activity that we do as a class; it forces me to develop numerous skills, such as critical thinking and time allocation. . . . It fosters an environment rich with creativity and innovation that invariably stimulates students. The independent research projects boost my self-confidence because I am genuinely excited about the topic and proud of the work I produce and share."

—GRETCHEN, GRADE 11

What Frameworks, Components, and Processes Support IBL?

This is not a book about Genius Hour, passion projects, and Makerspaces per se. We consider these to be curriculum models for IBL. These are learning designs that can and should be instituted in a school or classroom that values student agency. Minds greater than ours have already championed their use and explained their benefits. This book supports these models by outlining a universal framework (the eight-step IBL process) that aids the management of any form of interest-based learning and supports its coaching, assessment, and success.

To clarify these models, we define them here. Genius Hour originated in corporations and businesses that allocated time (e.g., 20% time) for employees to work on their own projects. In a school or classroom setting, teachers allocate classroom time for similar interest-based inquiry projects. Students explore any real-world interest with their teacher's support. Passion projects are interest-based inquiries that often culminate in a sharing session, product, or service. A Makerspace is a location in a classroom or school library that allows students with common or varied interests to come together to work on projects, especially those that involve technology and hands-on tasks. These students sometimes share equipment, provide support, and collaborate.

Regardless of the specific model selected by practitioners, we suggest that all forms of IBL can be represented by the IBL framework (see Figure 1, p. 7). We use the word *project* to describe an individual, partner, or small-group adventure that is guided by a specific aim. Lastly, we include the word *inquiry* to designate the purpose for an interest-based project. The foundation for IBL includes attention to its prerequisites and the developments of its shared vision. The process itself has eight different phases or steps that occur sequentially across the course of each child's project. These include:

1. finding interests;
2. focusing interests;
3. goal setting, developing inquiry questions, and mapping plans;
4. finding and managing resources;
5. researching, investigating, exploring, experimenting, and designing;
6. determining and designing products;
7. tapping potential audiences; and
8. reflecting, debriefing, and celebrating.

Embedded in every stage of the process are content, content literacy, and social-emotional learning standards, and the application of an aligned formative assessment system.

What Research Supports IBL?

There are at least three different types of research related to interests and interest-based learning. The first category of research seeks to describe interest and explain its origins, clarify the two different kinds of interests (i.e., situational and individual) to detail the process learners experience as they progress through interest's developmental stages, and document its impact on students' choices and future actions. We recommend that you review the work of Alexander et al. (2008) and Hidi (2006) for more detailed information. Dewey's (1913) seminal work is also worthy of attention.

The second type of research examines the influence of interest on student motivation. These studies strongly suggest that students achieve at higher levels when they are interested and engaged with a topic. Relevant researchers and experts include Schiefele and Csikszentmihalyi (1995) and Tomlinson et al. (1998).

The third type of relevant research measures the impact of various teaching strategies and influences on students' academic achievement. The chief source of these findings is the meta-analyses conducted and analyzed by Hattie (2009) using effect size, which can be used to measures the difference between a group that receives a given strategy or influence and a group that does not. Effect size calculations yield a decimal number that represents the amount of standard deviation difference between the two groups. Hattie considered an effect size of .40 or higher indicative of a strategy that positively enhances academic achievement beyond the boundaries of typical grade-level instruction. For easier interpretation, the effect size of a given influence can also be represented as a percentile difference. For example, a strategy that has an effect size of .40 is aligned with the 67th percentile. This percentile score means that the average person in the control group (who did not experience the strategy or influence) scored 66% lower than the average person in the experimental group (who received the strategy). We reviewed Hattie's research to identify strategies and influences that are likely to be present during the IBL process. The strategies, influences, and their effect sizes include self-efficacy (.82), scaffolding (.82), planning (.76), formative assessment (.70), feedback (.70), goal setting (.68), enrichment (.53), note-taking (.50), and self-motivation (.45).

If these strategies and influences are implemented with fidelity during interest-based learning opportunities, participating students are most likely to experience the related increase in academic achievement. These effect sizes, in and of themselves, are powerful reasons for initiating and investigating learning in our classrooms.

What Is the Relationship Between the IBL Framework and Current Inquiry Learning Models?

The framework for IBL described in this book is meant to complement and support educators' use of popular curriculum models, such as Genius Hour, passion projects, or Makerspaces. These three models, along with the more generic problem-based, project-based, and experiential learning paradigms, have similar, but not identical, features.

These models vary with regard to their purposes, goals, and organizational structures. Some emphasize creativity and design (e.g., Makerspaces), while others stress problem solving, research, and exploration. In some of these approaches, the teacher acts as the director of student learning, while other models suggest that the teacher serves as a coach or a passive observer. The timeline for such projects also varies from stipulated and fixed to open-ended. Third, topic selection may be teacher-directed or student-selected, firmly based on the subject matter for a specific course or wide-ranging and based solely on a student's questions and goals.

Some of these models do not expect an authentic product or audience from each participating student, and others emphasize these features. Other models integrate technology and incorporate different configurations related to choice, interest, group size, planning, problem solving, and analytical thinking. These models also differ with respect to their use of resources, audiences, and products. We do not advocate for one model over another. That decision should be made at the local level and based on a shared vision, schedule flexibility, time allocations, and resource budgets. We offer, instead, a universal process and framework that undergirds and strengthens the likelihood of success for any of these models.

Conclusion

You should now be able to define IBL and explain its rationale, goals, framework, and components. This chapter also explained the alignment between IBL and content knowledge and skill standards, 21st-century skills, and social-emotional learning standards. Lastly, this chapter provided a brief review of related research comparisons among current inquiry learning models. In the following two chapters, you will consider the foundational elements of IBL. In the next chapter, we turn attention to creating a shared vision for IBL with students.

CHAPTER 2

Ensuring a Strong Foundation

There are no secrets to success. It is the result of preparation, hard work, and learning from failure.

—Colin Powell

Can you remember a time when you realized that you were less than successful with an initiative because you hadn't known the conditions—early on—that were essential to your success? We surely remember lots of times when we did not investigate fully beforehand. We want to save you from having to experience that resulting sense of wasted time and frustration. In this chapter, we describe the nonnegotiables that are essential to the success of a classroom IBL initiative. Our caveat to you: If you are not confident that you have the elements outlined in this chapter in place and working smoothly, you should: (1) take a deep breath, (2) review the components carefully, (3) identify which elements need to be implemented or—most likely—to be tweaked, and (4) spend critical up-front time setting the stage for your future effective and triumphant work with IBL.

The prerequisites we describe in this chapter answer three of the Five Ws (Who? What? When? Where? Why?). The Five Ws are the foundation for any basic information gathering, whether part of a police investigation or journalism, and they are a formula for getting a complete story. The When? and Where? questions relate to the time available in the classroom, as well as its physical space and layout, and the Who? question relates to the new roles for the students, teachers, and knowledge.

We answered the What? (definition) and Why? (rationale) questions in the introduction and Chapter 1.

At the end of this chapter, you will be able to:

1. identify the physical attributes that are prerequisites of an IBL initiative, including sufficient time and classroom space;
2. enumerate several practical and easy-to-implement ideas to capture significant classroom time to support an IBL initiative;
3. explain the new roles for students, teachers, and knowledge in an IBL initiative;
4. inform other key players, including building administrators and parents, to ensure successful implementation;
5. explain significant educational theories that undergird interest-based learning; and
6. identify salient research that supports an IBL initiative.

Prerequisite 1: Physical Aspects

Sufficient Classroom Time

You must think us crazy to be suggesting that there's time available to initiate an IBL initiative. Many teachers' biggest concern is lack of classroom time to accomplish all that has to be done in a day, whether it is the amount of curriculum to cover, the demands from other new initiatives that have been adopted by the district, required state and local assessments, or lunch and specials, just to name a few. Teachers' most precious resource is time. But don't stop reading just yet! Our combined years in education suggest that there *is* enough classroom time, a claim that you might think is preposterous. Please give us a chance to provide some evidence.

As former classroom teachers with many years of experiences in regular and gifted education, we know about the range of learners in classrooms. Early on, we learned to use formative assessments to diagnose students' learning needs and subsequently tailor small-group instruction. Whether it was elementary, middle, or high school, we discovered that we could minimize the amount of large-group instruction that was required, learned how to use the membership of small groups to support learning, empowered students to take some responsibility for their own learning, and learned how to be a facilitator of all students' learning rather than the lecturer who had to do it all. The result? We worked just as hard, but we worked differently. And, as a result, we didn't always have to cover everything in the curriculum. Voila! Students were owning some of their learning, we were no longer feeling caught in a never-ending Catch-22, and we freed up a portion of classroom time because we no longer had to be the sage who had to teach everything to everybody.

Further, the Internet is replete with techniques and advice for how to save classroom time. We conducted a search with the key terms "saving classroom time" and "how to" and we retrieved 557,000 results in .51 seconds. There are thousands of ideas for saving classroom time. With that said, you, who may already feel overburdened, do *not* have enough time to sift and curate the best ideas for your classrooms Thus, we have done that for you, and the most effective ideas are outlined in Table 1.

With these techniques available to you, don't forget to seek overlaps with other like-minded colleagues, whether they are librarians working on Makerspaces, science teachers working on experiments, or social studies teachers working on project-based learning or Legacy Projects. If your school librarian is already covering research skills, you do not need to cover the same material. If your teammate in social studies is covering how to develop inquiry questions, you do not need to spend so much time on it with your students. Similarly, if your teammate in science is covering how to assess the credibility of resources, then you likely do not need to spend as much time on it as you thought. Your colleagues will help you capture time, and your collaboration will enhance the impact of IBL and serve to galvanize your team and/or grade-level colleagues.

The need to capture classroom time is nothing new. In 1991, a national commission was established to conduct a comprehensive review of the relationship between time and learning in the nation's classrooms. In 1994, the Education Commission of the States's publication *Prisoners of Time* was released. Sadly, little has changed since—except that today there are even higher expectations for all learners. Thus, the following words of advice from the 1994 report continue to echo and propel work with IBL: "Use time in new, different and better ways, and reinvent schools around learning, not time" (p. 30).

With these parting words from that visionary report in mind, return to our original claim that you can capture enough teaching time to successfully implement IBL for a portion of time each week: 10%, 15%, or even 20%. If you are confident that you could capture a portion of your instructional time, you may be good to go. If you realize that you are not yet confident, all is not lost. In fact, we are glad that you acknowledge your need to slow down. Quite simply, all you may need to do is research and refine several of the time-saving strategies in Table 1 to help you free up the time you need to feel comfortable allocating a portion of your instructional time to IBL. In the end, you are helping to ensure that you will eventually have the necessary preconditions in place to be successful with your implementation of IBL.

More important is your own mindset when it comes to classroom time. You must ask yourself: "Have I done what I can to prepare students for the 21st century?" "Have I done 'test prep' or 'life prep'?" You are mistaken if you have kept the focus solely on test prep. A rich, robust, transformative, and personally empower-

TABLE 1
Strategies for Saving Classroom Time

Strategy	Description	Examples/References
Teach to the Standards	Eliminate activities, assessments, projects, and assignments that do not match the learning targets for the standards.	See Chapters 1, 7, 8, and 10.
Preassessment	Administer preassessments aligned with the standards; use the data to target pinpointed instruction only to those students who need it. Well-aligned and short preassessments at the start of and throughout curriculum units can save classroom time by eliminating unnecessary whole-group instruction.	See http://www.ascd.org/ publications/educational_ leadership/dec13/vol71/num04/ Differentiation@_It_Starts_ with_Pre-Assessment.aspx.
Teach From "Bell to Bell"	Use every minute of classroom time.	Creative use of storage space, classroom routines, and student understanding (i.e., expectations that they use their time effectively) will contribute to captured instructional time.
Classroom Management	There are literally hundreds of websites that offer creative ways to manage the classroom and that will keep the focus on instruction.	See https://www.scholastic. com/teachers/articles/ teaching-content/18-classroom-management-hacks.
Classroom Organization	Post to-do lists, instructions, and anchor charts, and make resources readily available to students.	Use resources like Google Classroom or class folder systems to provide students with instructions and materials in order to minimize time spent explaining and disseminating information.
Meeting Learning Goals	Record instructional reteach lessons for students to view on their own time.	Prerecord standard recovery workshop model lessons for students who need a reteach/ refresher on specific standards and make them available, along with necessary materials and resources, as needed.

TABLE 1, CONTINUED

Strategy	Description	Examples/References
Classroom Engagement	Share responsibility for learning.	"Three Before Me," a commonly used management technique, helps create expectations around classroom routines and encourages students to take ownership of their learning and interactions. It also saves teacher and instructional time.
Work Collaboratively With Colleagues	Reach out to colleagues who teach to standards and aligned curriculum modules that are similar to yours. Agree to share responsibility for teaching, thereby reinforcing each other and saving instructional time.	We allude to this strategy in this chapter and Chapter 8.

ing 21st-century education gives students recursive opportunities to: (1) engage in rich and challenging opportunities to talk with each other; (2) actively and enthusiastically problem solve on multifaceted, consequential, and "messy" tasks; and (3) present their findings to interested real-world stakeholders, thereby impacting their community. This monumental challenge can be successfully navigated *only* by educators with a positive mindset about the elasticity of the school day and about students who will live in a future educators don't yet know.

Also note that when you implement an IBL program, you are *not* supporting the notion that students become "free-range" entities. Rather—and regardless of students' self-selected content—their work will always be tethered to a wide range of grade-level content standards, 21st-century skills, or social-emotional learning tenets. We place such a heavy emphasis on the integration of standards and skills with an IBL initiative, that standards are—once again—addressed in the chapters dealing with making a management plan, resources, and products (Chapters 7, 8, and 10, respectively).

Sufficient Classroom Space

Sufficient classroom space is crucial, as students will need space in which to work, including their desks or tables; in-class computer terminals (if they are available); places to store papers, notes, books, and other resources; flash drives;

product-related realia; and other types of investigative equipment, such as cameras and recorders. For many classroom teachers, this space is not an issue. With that said, you still need to think about and plan ahead for how space will be allocated.

Further, note how important it is that IBL moves beyond the classroom's traditional walls. More space can be opened up if you begin to think about how other school and community spaces can be utilized: the library, music room, and art room space; other town facilities, buildings, and outdoor areas; and central office locations and facilities, just to name a few.

Teachers who move from classroom to classroom may have an issue with classroom space required by an IBL initiative. If you are an itinerant teacher, you will need to plan collaboratively with other like-minded professional and administrators to ensure that you will have the space that you need.

Prerequisite 2: New Roles for Students, Knowledge, and the Teacher

Now that you have a clear understanding of the physical requirements for success, turn your attention to the second prerequisite: changes that IBL necessitates in the roles of the key stakeholders. These new roles are equally important as the physical requirements. We believe that there are many newer teachers who think that IBL is a new idea. Consider, however, Dewey's (1938) *Experience and Education* and Kirkpatrick's (1918) essay "The Project Method." We also remember Renzulli's (1982) memorable article "What Makes a Problem Real." In his pioneering work to define what qualitatively differentiated learning looks like, he examined and defined anew the role of the student, knowledge, and the teacher. The purpose of his analysis was singular: to forward an "acid test" to determine whether learning was truly differentiated.

IBL, implemented with fidelity, can be distinguished from other classroom learning by Renzulli's (1982) acid test: the roles of students, knowledge, and the teacher. Students have traditionally been cast as learners of prescribed lessons and doers of learning activities that have already been answered. In the IBL framework, students are much more involved. They choose their topics (within reason), become firsthand inquirers, and often produce a real product that they present to an audience other than the teacher.

The role of knowledge also morphs. Traditionally, content knowledge was acquired in a linear fashion by students, stored away for some future use, and usually emerged from a textbook or other academic source. In the IBL framework, knowledge is determined by students' self-selected problems as they unfold, students use their knowledge to act upon aspects of their problem in a cyclical fashion, and knowledge comes from many different real sources.

The new roles of the student and knowledge impact the role of the teacher. No longer totally responsible for creating and implementing curriculum and exercises—a master of all things curriculum—the teacher becomes the managerial assistant to students. The teacher assists students with defining and focusing problems of interest, locating and acquiring resources across the community, identifying potentially powerful product formats, locating potential audiences who can provide authentic evaluations, and providing feedback and questions.

We hear you asking, "You want me to do *what*?" Indeed, we ask that teachers reinvent themselves for IBL classroom time. If you have a robust growth mindset, you will make the conversion easily; in fact, it will come naturally. Or you might have to begin transitioning into this new role by being mindful of the necessary changes so that you grow into them until they become natural behavior during this special classroom time. Your successful metamorphosis will allow students to take more responsibility for and ownership of their learning—a long sought-after educational goal. On the other hand, following the logic of the argument presented here, you might be thinking that we are being sacrilegious to suggest that all students do what high-achieving young people traditionally have done. We understand your thinking and propose this line of logic because all students should have the opportunity to become firsthand inquirers for a small portion of their time in school.

Prerequisite 3: Informing Key Stakeholders

At this point, we hope you have a firm understanding of the physical and role prerequisites for successfully implementing IBL. Beyond the physical and role prerequisites, we will now look now at the two remaining tasks that will help to ensure your success: informing parents and building administrators.

Administrators

We are fond of the articles written by Karen Rogers in the 1990s about the effectiveness of acceleration practices (e.g., Rogers & Kimpston, 1992). What struck us back then was the overall excellence, merit, and advanced research practices that characterized Rogers's work, as well as her sense of ethics and honesty. As a result, we felt confident that acceleration practices—implemented with fidelity—would have a payoff for students and educators. And, indeed, we needed to feel confident. At that time, acceleration was a lightning rod in the field. Reactions from opponents were overwhelming and intimidating. Colangelo et al. (2004) wrote a report, *A Nation Deceived: How Schools Hold Back America's Brightest Students*, to respond to the rising national sentiment regarding the acceleration practices recommended by the field. By itself, the title of the report provides an instant glimpse into the fervor of the time period. Why do we mention this time period? Quite simply, educators now face a similar situation with respect to IBL. Today's classroom teachers are being asked to sacrifice what they intuitively know is good for their students (and what the research shows) in exchange for appeasing outside forces. Thus, you need to be highly effective when you communicate with your administrators about an IBL initiative.

In your initial letter or e-mail to administrators seeking approval for your venture (see Resource 1: Sample Letter to Administration), you will need to cite reputable research, as well as foundational educational theories, as a rationale for incorporating IBL into your classroom practices. In today's school districts that increasingly call for rigorous and research-based practices, educators can no longer afford to cite merely testimonials and/or the number of "likes" that float about on the Internet for innovative approaches to education. Further, you will need to assure administrators that classroom time will not be lost; in fact, your classroom time will be used more efficiently to ensure the fidelity of implementation. Administrators are much more likely to back your work if they understand how IBL is grounded in theory and research, is aligned to standards, and holds the promise to positively impact your students, your colleagues, and the community.

See Appendix B for a summary of the most salient education theories that support IBL, as well as current empirical research on the impact of choice in the classroom. The research provided in Appendix B is slightly different that the research cited in Chapter 1. Sources in Appendix B have been curated because they are either theoretically sound or empirically based, and are especially pertinent for building and central office leaders.

Parents

In our educational careers, we have had the great fortune to travel to all corners of the country. Meeting educators has been inspiring because we learn so much with each visit about the culture and customs of the place. While travelling in the Deep South years ago, we were introduced to the saying: "If Momma ain't happy, then no one is gonna be happy." How true this saying is across all contexts. It is

RESOURCE 1
Sample Letter to Administration

Dear _____,

It is nearly fall, and I am excited to begin our next school year together. I hope your year is off to a smooth start.

Over the last few months, I have read and researched about interest-based learning (IBL), and a central tenet of this instructional strategy is student choice. I believe IBL holds a great deal of promise for our students. Implementation of this strategy will promote student motivation, time on task, and enjoyment of school. At the same time, IBL will make me more efficient in my teaching and not compromise my ongoing work to cover all of my required grade-level standards.

Interest-based learning is based on three current educational theories. Additionally, current meta-analyses about the use of classroom choice suggest that students who are offered choice for some portion of their school week may experience heightened motivation, persist longer at tasks, and complete higher quality work in their chosen area.

I would like to meet with you to discuss these ideas and my implementation of IBL in the coming year. In anticipation of our meeting, I am attaching a couple of brief articles.

I look forward to hearing back from you.

Sincerely,

_____

especially relevant here because parents need to know what's happening in their children's classrooms so that they can be supportive of your efforts, as well as their children's efforts, with IBL. To that end, we have drafted a sample letter home that you can copy or adapt to your own purposes (see Resource 2: Sample Letter to Parents). Whatever letter or e-mail you send, consider having administrators review it before the beginning of school so that you can get it into the hands of parents and/ or guardians before your implementation begins.

Conclusion

In this chapter we identified the critical prerequisites for a successful venture into IBL learning: a mindset that you have sufficient time, appropriate classroom space, and the support of both building administrators and parents. The next chapter focuses on vision making and sharing, an essential process that builds ownership for the IBL initiative.

Dear Parent(s),

Hello. My name is _____ , and I am your child's _____ teacher. I'm writing to you because I have something exciting I want to share with you regarding our classroom. Over the following marking periods, we are going to be using one day a week to engage in students' self-selected interests.

The idea behind this initiative is simple: I want my students to be engaged in work that they find important and personally rewarding and take greater ownership of their learning. I will be guiding them through all aspects of their projects, and my goals for our work together are to:

- × increase my understanding of your child's learning interests,
- × increase my students' motivation for academic learning, and
- × enhance the school's relationship with parents in the community.

This is an exciting venture for me and my students. I want to assure you that our weekly time is not a free-for-all and that learning is of paramount importance. All projects will be based within our content standards, and students will be held accountable for the deadlines that they create. To that end, I would encourage you to ask your children about their projects, talk with them about what they're working on, and support their initiative and diligence. Not only will it help them be mindful of what they're working on, but also it will give them a chance to share the incredible work that they're doing.

I look forward to speaking with you more about our venture anytime, especially at any of our scheduled open houses. If you have any information about your child's emerging interests, please let me know. Feel free to reach out to me at _____ (phone) or _____ (e-mail).

Sincerely,

_____

Sample Letter to Parents

_____

CHAPTER 3

Vision Making
and Sharing

> The future is not a result of choices among alternative paths offered by the present, but a place that is created—created first in mind and will, created next in activity. The future is not some place we are going to, but one we are creating. The paths to it are not found but created, and the activity of creating them changes both the maker and the destination. (Schaar, 1981, p. 321)

Until now, you have considered, analyzed, and ensured that the prerequisites are in place to launch your IBL initiative. With the prerequisites firmly in place, it is time to turn your attention to your students. This section of the playbook is focused on beginning activities with young people: vision making and sharing.

Perhaps you are beginning your IBL initiative at the start of the school year, midway through the school year, or even toward the end of the academic year. You can enter into IBL at any time. The logical order in which you complete the steps toward successful implementation is what's important. As you recall from the introduction, vision making is a critical foundational step of IBL. As such, we are devoting an entire chapter to it because it contains lots of practical suggestions for you to use.

After reading this chapter, you will be able to:

1. explain the importance of vision making and vision sharing with students;
2. identify and use 2–5 videos to introduce IBL that showcase real-world student projects and that can be used as exemplars with existing students (e.g.,

YouTube videos, TED talks listed in Table 2), or identify former students who completed successful IBL projects in previous years and who are willing to be guest speakers in your classroom to share their project experiences; and

3. share your vision for the upcoming work in such a way that it becomes a compelling invitation and visualization for everyone in the class.

Vision Making and Sharing: A Big Deal?

You might be wondering why you should begin your work with students by sharing your vision for an IBL initiative. You might just be saying, "Just tell the students what they are going to do and get on with it! My class time is too short already!"

We beg to differ, as does Schaar (1981), the futurist whose quotation is featured at the opening of this chapter. We believe that high-quality time on vision making and sharing with students will help to ensure the success of the IBL initiative. Let us first make an important distinction, our reason for spending time on this critical step, and then provide you with the how-tos.

Sharing a vision does not mean adopting someone else's vision. Reliance on someone else's vision perpetuates dependence and conformity. And what happens to visions when they are merely adopted and never truly owned by members in any organization? Prematurely, these imposed visions die because they were never really part of the culture.

How should you avoid the premature death of your IBL initiative? To ensure deep ownership requires meaningful engagement and collaboration with students about what they are about to undertake. This collective vision building, described in the following section, is purposively designed to increase clarity, enthusiasm, agency, communication, and commitment from all involved in the IBL initiative. Put simply, when everybody truly owns something, they readily focus their energies, accept responsibility, and care about it. And mind you, IBL is dramatically different from students' experiences in the traditional classroom. With IBL, they are owning a corner of the curriculum—a far cry from a doer of teacher-prepared lessons and worksheets! Thus, students must operate with a sense of shared vision about their IBL involvement.

Inviting Students Into IBL

Now, to the how-tos. Do you remember or have you heard of that 1950s television show *Name That Tune*? It was a classic game show on NBC and CBS that put two contestants of various ages against each other to test their knowledge of songs. The centerpiece of the series was an orchestra, which would play parts of songs for the contestants to see who could recognize them—in the fewest notes possible. In a similar way, we believe you can invite students into an IBL initiative in three easy steps—or notes, if you will.

Step 1: Generate Curiosity and Interest

The first step is to get students curious about IBL. Common techniques include, but are not limited to: (1) participation in an activity that has a clear and direct bridge to the learning target, (2) a discrepant event—related to the learning target—that piques curiosity, (3) establishing a clear connection to prior knowledge and an explanation for how the upcoming information will extend learning, and (4) showcasing real-world examples that illustrate how the new learning is applied in the real world, just to name a few (Lancelot, 1944). Lancelot explained that these techniques all rely on natural human impulses, teachers should always integrate them into their teaching to enhance student learning, and this appeal was the cornerstone of his interest approach to teaching.

The videos listed in Table 2 can spark curiosity and interest among your students as they approach IBL. Note that all of the young people featured in the videos have accomplished remarkable things. In no way do we want your students to think they have to take on projects of such magnitude. We showcase these examples not only because they are inspirational, but also because they are riveting.

Of course, you have the opportunity to employ other ways to appeal to students' sense of wonder and curiosity. If former students completed IBL projects and they still attend school in your building, invite one or two to be guest speakers and talk about their experiences. Alternatively, you might have wisely stored away exemplar projects from previous years. If you have two or three saved away, this would be the ideal time to share them with your current students.

If you decide to show any of the videos included in Table 2, invite any guest students from previous years who are willing to share their projects, or showcase one or two past projects yourself, begin by overviewing the few (2–4) that you share with students. You can tell your students that young people—like themselves—driven by a passion completed the projects. Provide two focus questions for each project that

TABLE 2
List of Possible TED Talks and YouTube Videos

Title	URL	Duration	Summary
"Being Young and Making an Impact"	https://www.ted.com/talks/natalie_warne_being_young_and_making_an_impact	12:47	At 17, Natalie Warne learned about the Invisible Children Project, a campaign to rescue Ugandan children from Joseph Kony's child armies. She led a nationwide campaign for the project.
"My Invention That Made Peace With the Lions"	https://www.ted.com/talks/richard_turere_a_peace_treaty_with_the_lions	7:20	Richard Turere is a young teenage inventor who shares the solar-powered solution he designed to safely scare lions away from his Maasai community to protect cattle.
"A 12-Year-Old App Developer"	https://www.ted.com/talks/thomas_suarez_a_12_year_old_app_developer	4:40	Thomas Suarez, age 12, develops iPhone apps and games, and uses his skills to help other kids become developers.
"Bluegrass Virtuosity From . . . New Jersey"	https://www.ted.com/talks/sleepy_man_banjo_boys_bluegrass_virtuosity_from_new_jersey/transcript	8:47	Young brothers Jonny, Robbie, and Tommy Mizzone from New Jersey perform and create their own bluegrass compositions.
"6-Year-Old Sophie Cruz Gives Amazing Speech in D.C."	https://www.youtube.com/watch?v=LeX9vuRY4FE	3:06	Sophie Cruz, age 6, who is the daughter of undocumented immigrants, talks about the importance of people coming together as one.
"Iqbal Masih Documentary"	https://www.youtube.com/watch?v=UStGtNe6VJ0	6:55	Iqbal Masih was a Pakistani Christian boy who became an activist against child labor and abuse.
"5 Years Into Water Crisis, Little Miss Flint Hasn't Given Up	GMA"	https://www.youtube.com/watch?v=7tvm8A0J3lg	3:08	Mari Copeny, age 6, is an environmental activist who helped to publicize and assist in solving the Flint, MI, water crisis.

you showcase, giving students time at the conclusion of each to write brief answers to two targeted questions, such as:

1. What was the student's interest that you saw in the video or presentation?
2. In what ways are you like the featured student?

Step 2: Debrief With Students

After you have concluded each video and/or sharing from other students, debrief your students. To ensure engagement among all of your students, provide them with 3–4 minutes to talk about their answers in small groups in a think-pair-share. Once students have had their small-group discussions, have them share among the whole group. Some student understandings that you seek for a successful IBL journey include:

× everyone has interests;
× each young person had the chance to do something with their interest;
× each child had support to continue with their interest;
× each young person was a "mover and shaker," and they made a big difference for themselves and others;
× each of your students is a "mover and shaker;"
× some projects were relatively short, while others were of a longer duration; and
× some projects have an enormous impact, and others have less of an impact, but impact is not an attribute of success.

Step 3: Share Your Vision

Following your debriefing, connect the discussion to your students' unique set of interests. You can use questions such as any of the following:

× What would you be doing now if you weren't in school and could be doing anything you wanted?
× What would happen if you could work on a project that you love for a portion of time each week in school?
× If you were a "mover and shaker," what would be your mission?

"Wait. You mean, really? You mean I might be able to write about street bikes for this project? Did I hear you right? I have never, ever had a teacher tell me that I could use what I am doing outside of class for class."

—SIMON, GRADE 4

Subsequently, you can transition into your vision for the upcoming IBL work. Your vision sharing to the class might illuminate any of the following. Throughout IBL, students will be able to:

1. choose a topic about which they are passionate;
2. choose to work alone or with 2–3 other students interested in the same topic;
3. share their work with the class and/or others in the school and community;
4. work in class on their self-selected project one day a week;
5. talk with other students about their projects and their progress;
6. understand that some projects will take longer than others;
7. understand that, if they finish before others, they will have the opportunity to pursue another project;
8. understand that your role will be a managerial assistant—they will do the work, and you will support and guide them;
9. check in with you regularly;
10. use different kinds of resources that you will help them locate;
11. write and keep their own notes about their progress to journal prompts that you will share with them;
12. be responsible for monitoring their own progress; and
13. report regularly about their progress to you and the class.

CASE STUDIES
Andrea and Pablo

Some students might be so enthusiastic about the possibilities outlined in your vision that they will feel compelled to share their interests immediately and without prompting. Such is the case with Andrea and Pablo. Andrea is a sixth-grade student who is very socially aware, has a range and intensity of

---

emotions typical of an 11-year-old, displays an ability—uncharacteristic of preadolescents—to see people and events from a variety of perspectives, and has an abiding interest in all aspects of iMovie. Her fifth-grade teacher mentioned at the end the previous school year that she just couldn't get Andrea to "get off the iMovie kick." Every project Andrea completed had something to do with iMovie. Thus, it was not surprising that Andrea, when you were walking by her desk, asked in a whisper, "Can I do a project that involves iMovie?"

Pablo is a much quieter sixth grader. You have noted that he seems to be so much more engaged in class when scientific topics are being discussed. Additionally, several times in class he has expressed opinions about environmental topics that were beyond his years. You have said to yourself that his interest in science and social activism is something you need to investigate and help him channel.

Conclusion

Jack Scharr, the futurist—whose quotation opened this chapter—is absolutely right. You are, indeed, engaged in creating the future. This vision of collaboration, self-directed learning, and products shared with audiences will not only become part of your classroom, but also feature prominently in the 21st-century workplace.

Sharing your vision with students for the IBL initiative is an important first step. Done well, vision sharing increases clarity, enthusiasm, agency, communication, and commitment from all involved. When everybody truly owns something, they readily accept responsibility, focus their energies, and care about it. It is not a bad payoff for spending a little extra time up front!

Now that we have finished with our discussion of foundational elements (i.e., ensuring prerequisites are in place and vision building), we will turn our attention to the formative assessment system that we are proposing for your work with IBL. As you remember from the introduction, we are placing it up front for two reasons. The formative assessment system we are proposing is so critical to the success of an IBL initiative that it needs to be one among the first chapters. Second, charting students' progress and timely feedback should always be in the background of all that you do. Accurate formative assessment of student progress, coupled with feedback, will help to propel each of your students over the finish line.

CHAPTER 4

Measuring the Impact of Interest-Based Learning

Standardized testing is at cross purposes with many of the most important purposes of public education. It doesn't measure big-picture learning, critical thinking, perseverance, problem-solving, creativity or curiosity, yet those are the qualities great teaching brings out in a student.

—Randi Weingarten

Measure what is measurable and make measurable what is not so.

—Galileo Galilei

This chapter covers the definition, role, benefits, and process of formative assessment throughout the IBL process. We emphasize the importance of student-friendly goal statements and assessment criteria, and provide templates and examples of the various criteria that might be used to measure progress and growth. Authentic evidence is another critical aspect of the formative assessment process, and this chapter offers examples of the various kinds of work products that address this function. We follow with an explanation and example of effective feedback components and strategies for teacher-to-student and student-to-teacher feedback. The last portion of this chapter addresses the management of formative assessment within the IBL process. Several templates for conferences and formative assessment are provided, as well as tools for record-keeping and note-taking. Potential conference topics and feedback guidelines are included.

After reading this chapter, you will be able to:

1. define formative assessment,
2. clarify the role of formative assessment within the IBL process,
3. explain the benefits of formative assessment within IBL,
4. describe the process and facets of a comprehensive formative assessment system, and
5. specify the implementation and management of formative assessment during the IBL process.

What Is Formative Assessment?

Formative assessment is a multifaceted process used by educators and students during the learning process. It is typically informal, involving observations, work samples, conversations, or a look at students' work in progress. Formative assessment involves the development and use of student-friendly learning targets (goals) that collectively address each specific aspect of a learning standard, goal, or objective; student-friendly success criteria; and the identification of the evidence, data, behavior, products, or tasks that will be used to measure progress toward each learning target (Moss & Brookhart, 2019).

As a result of the formative assessment process, students and teachers collaboratively generate feedback. This feedback focuses on the collected and available evidence or work products and actions, and compares it to the learning target and success criteria. Used regularly, such feedback provides students with suggestions and support for moving closer to each target. Feedback provided habitually during the IBL process also allows students and teachers to make appropriate adjustments that will enhance the likelihood that students reach their learning goals.

For example, if a student is interested in finding out if or how their Florida town protects sea turtle nests, the learning targets for this process would include each of the IBL steps and probably also integrate goals related to biology content, reasoning, literacy, and social-emotional development. Each of these targets would have criteria for measuring the quality of the student's work, and the formative assessment process would occur two to four times during the life of the project. Feedback from the formative assessment might be used to adjust the focus of the student's learning question, the nature of the student's resources, or the self-management strategies the student is using during the course of their project.

What Is the Role of Formative Assessment in IBL?

Formative assessment fulfills three different roles within the IBL process. First and foremost, formative assessment acts as a magnifying glass. If attended to early in the IBL process, a comprehensive formative assessment system helps educators and students concentrate their attention on the "L" portion of the IBL acronym. Many students' impulse is to jump immediately to thoughts of an interest-based product or topic. That is natural and to be expected, but if you want your parents and administrators to value and respect the valuable time needed for IBL, you need to honor their expectations for student learning. Attention to the preliminary aspects of formative assessment forces educators and students to closely examine their state content and literacy standards, their social-emotional learning standards, and the 21st-century expectations for problem solving, reasoning, and leadership. Like a magnifying glass, a closer look at these standards helps educators and students link the relevant standards with students' interest-based project goals.

Second, formative assessment assumes the role of a three-dimensional measuring tool, such as a weather station, which measures multiple aspects (e.g., temperature, humidity, and wind direction) of the weather. In a similar fashion, formative assessment measures multiple aspects of a student's evidence of learning (i.e., data, notes, work-in-progress, drafts, designs, diagrams, behaviors, and reflections) through its use of three different tools: students' learning targets, their success criteria, and the agreed-upon levels of proficiency. Used together, these three components allow evaluators to transect the evidence of learning to measure growth and identify the aspects of each target that still need to be learned.

Third, when formative assessment incorporates feedback, it assumes the role of a coach. A coach uses evidence from game films to identify missing, erroneous, or substandard aspects of an athletes' performance during a given play. These imperfect elements are communicated to the athlete (not always in a loving and respectful demeanor) in anticipation of enhanced performance in the near future.

During the formative assessment process, feedback acts as a coach for student researchers and designers. Success criteria are used to measure evidence and to identify missing or subpar evidence, thereby identifying the next steps for project work or revision. Assuming that the student is part of the feedback process, and not just its recipient, the likelihood of growth and progress increases, thereby fulfilling the major purpose for formative assessment and feedback.

Formative assessment is a vital aspect of the IBL process. Its three different roles, as a magnifying glass, a weather station, and a coach, provide the assessment process with the necessary next steps that students need to take to move closer to their learning targets.

Benefits of Formative Assessment in IBL

Consider the reality of having 25 students, each of whom is participating in four to 15 different projects. We know that you may be asking some very real questions: "How do I possibly manage so many different projects going on at the same time?" or "How do I keep track of all of this work?"

Project variety and quantity are commonplace when implementing IBL. Remembering which students are doing what projects is important, as is a teacher's need for management and record-keeping. (We address the time-saving benefits of small-group projects in Chapter 2 and the management of IBL projects in Chapter 7.) For now, and in this chapter, take a closer look at the role that formative assessment plays in the quality of students' IBL projects.

There are at least three reasons to include formative assessment within the IBL process. First, when formative assessment is properly implemented and coupled with clear learning targets (student-friendly and well understood), success criteria, and feedback, it enhances the likelihood that each student will achieve their learning goals. As early as 1994, Wiggins endorsed the use of formative assessment as a tool for providing educators, administrators, and parents with more evidence, thus allowing an enhanced and comprehensive picture of learning progress. Later, in 2012, Hattie's meta-analyses found an average effect size of .48 for formative assessment, a .68 effect size for clear goals, and a .70 effect size for feedback—all evidence of significant impact on achievement. Formative assessment increases the likelihood that more students will achieve meaningful learning during the course of IBL. In turn, this demonstrated achievement provides evidence to support educators' claim that the IBL process is a valid use of valuable school time.

Timeliness is the second reason to implement formative assessment within the IBL process. The very nature of formative assessment means that it occurs often and throughout the learning process. It informs the teacher when learning is or is not progressing as intended. This is what distinguishes formative assessment from summative assessment. The repetitive and timely aspect of formative assessment provides opportunities for midcourse corrections; it catches gaps and misunderstandings before the learning opportunity ends (Hattie, 2009).

Timeliness means that you can use formative assessment as an early alert system to counter many of the issues you may have experienced with independent study projects that run aground because no one was monitoring student work. Imagine a student who isn't truly invested in his topic, or another child who is having trouble locating the resources she needs to answer her learning questions. The inclusion of formative assessment means that you can intervene and help students redirect their projects or brainstorm to locate just the right person to provide the tool or equipment students need.

This is especially relevant when students are new to IBL or may only work on their projects once a week. Memory lapses, forgotten materials, bouts of disorganization, and a tendency to flit from topic to topic without moving through all of the stages of an interest-based learning project are common phenomena for novices. Formative assessment reveals these issues quickly. Follow-up actions, such as coaching, scaffolding, direct instruction, collaboration with another student, or intervention, are the natural result of such evidence-based alerts.

The development of students' intrapersonal skills, attitudes, and dispositions is the third reason to incorporate formative assessment with IBL. As students share their work-in-progress and incrementally meet each of their learning targets, both you and your students can readily see and measure their learning growth. The formative assessment and feedback process acknowledges the positive impact of their self-management skills and intrinsic motivation. Coupled with reflection conversations about growth mindsets and self-efficacy, students are more likely to recognize the impact of their efforts on their own personal development, potentially influencing their future decisions and behaviors. When students have the opportunity to draft their own targets and success criteria (often with the teacher's support), using kid-friendly language, the targets become clearer and more personal. As a result, both agency and ownership improve.

The Formative Assessment Process

A comprehensive formative assessment system for IBL contains several, interrelated components (see Figure 2). They include the following:

1. **Content standards explain the essential knowledge, skills, reasoning, applications, and dispositions students are expected to learn within each academic area.** They define and focus the learning goals for curriculum and student work. Examples include the CCSS, the NGSS, the College, Career, and Civic Life (C3) Social Studies Framework from the NCSS, and many states' social-emotional, art, music, physical education, and 21st-century learning goals. In order to enhance the integrity and worthiness of students' research and design work, all IBL educators should have

FIGURE 2

Components of the IBL Formative Assessment System

Interest-Based Learning Goal + State Standards,
21st-Century Skills, and SEL Tenets

Identification of Student-Friendly Learning Targets
(One Target for Each Phase of the IBL Process)

Development of Student-Friendly Success Criteria

Development of 2–4 Student-Friendly Proficiency Levels

Student and Teacher Agreement About Relevant Evidence of Learning

Formative Assessment Evidence Review (Conference or Conversation)

Decision Regarding Proficiency Level With Each Target

Feedback and Decisions About Next Steps

the opportunity to consider how and which of these standards have a prominent place within their students' projects.

2. **Learning targets are statements that focus on one essential piece of knowledge, or a singular concept, skill, application, or disposition within a given interest area or standard.** Learning targets written in student-friendly language describe what learners are expected to understand or be able to do over the course of their IBL project (e.g., "I can find resources that help me answer my questions about sea turtle nests."). Each project's targets are typically organized and addressed in a logical sequence that aligns with the IBL process. Targets may also include student learning

of content, SEL, and 21st-century standards. To engage students and support their ownership of the learning goals, the goals must be clearly articulated. Brief conversations about learning targets help students understand the relevance and nature of each target. Each learning target becomes the focus for IBL work, formative assessment, feedback, and further work.

3. **Success criteria are the indicators that specify the desired qualities for students' work toward the learning target.** Criteria are critical for measuring progress during formative assessment, and they are also used during feedback conferences to chart the next steps. Criteria should be well-aligned to the target, collaboratively developed with students, and written in student-friendly language.

4. **Evidence of learning includes the research notes, lists of resources, designs, plans, behaviors, products, assignments, and demonstrations that serve as evidence of a student's current proficiency with the learning target.** Students and educators use relevant evidence and the target's success criteria to measure learning progress. Of course, these work products are considered drafts, amendable and subject to feedback, intervention, and resubmission.

5. **Proficiency levels reflect the proportion of the success criteria that are represented in the evidence of understanding.** Their related proficiency scales (e.g., beginning, basic, proficient, advanced, etc.) are typically included in rubrics and checklists.

6. **A user-friendly record-keeping system is crucial for the management of students' IBL projects, and formative assessment data become a natural part of those records.** Hattie's (2012) analysis indicated that shared, clear, and formative record-keeping has an average .52 effect size on student achievement. Each student's entries should identify the learning targets, their current proficiency levels, and coded or brief notes related to feedback and follow-through. Tools such as Excel or Google Docs provide an efficient way to record this quantitative and narrative information. Using the "split-cell" function, the rows can be used to list the class roster and the topic of each student's IBL project. The columns can list each phase of the IBL process as well as the related content, SEL, literacy, and 21st-century learning goals. The cells themselves can list the proficiency level with each target, and the "Notes" function can be used to record narrative information about feedback and follow-up. During formative assessment, and the IBL process in particular, student work is almost always in development, so expectations for score revision are commonplace.

7. **Feedback provides a written or oral summary of the evaluation process.** The most effective feedback involves student self-report and includes a description of the learning target, its criteria, and an appraisal of the

extent to which the evidence aligns with the proficiency expectations and success criteria. It also describes the next steps a student should consider to reach each learning target. The most effective formative assessment systems expect shared ownership of the process between teacher and student.

8. **Response to feedback is a process that works similarly to Response to Intervention.** RtI provides reading, math, and behavioral mediation for struggling learners using a variety of instructional approaches. Then, educators use formative assessment to measure the impact of the selected strategy on growth trajectory and achievement. As needed, educators make modifications to the schedule and strategies to produce greater growth and achievement. Feedback that follows an IBL formative assessment works in the same way. It attempts to intervene in the student's IBL process by providing coaching and suggested actions, strategies, steps, and resources that a student should consider in order to move closer to or achieve their target. How students respond to the feedback is another matter. The classroom climate, mutual respect, and rapport between student and teacher play a significant part in predicting student response to feedback, as do student self-efficacy, motivation, and drive. In the more student-centered classrooms, the students themselves identify their learning gaps and indicate their willingness to rework and revise their IBL tasks and assessment evidence. Of course, time must be made available in the IBL schedule to support such redirection, coaching, and resubmission work.

Incorporating and Managing Formative Assessment During IBL

The eight components of formative assessment discussed in the last section are part of every aspect of the IBL process. For that reason, formative assessment is represented as one of the surrounding circles in the IBL framework (see Figure 1, p. 7). As we explain how teachers can manage formative assessment throughout the IBL process, we will reference several students' projects. Table 3 contains these examples. Evident from the chart, the projects vary by grade level, topic, and goal.

As explained previously, the formative assessment process begins as soon as students have selected their learning question or goal. As with formative assessment in the academic arena, there are three crucial aspects that link formative assessment with enhanced achievement during an IBL initiative. These vital components include the use of relevant and student-friendly learning targets, assessment criteria, and proficiency levels. All three are used in concert to measure and

TABLE 3
Examples of Student IBL Goals

Sample IBL Goals and Questions			
Grade Level	Student Name	Focused Interest Area	Learning Goal or Question
K	Jamal	Engineering	I want to see if I can use those blocks over there to make the Tappan Zee Bridge.
1	Fredo	Music	I want to learn to play music.
2	Esteban	Chemistry	I want to learn about science experiments and show them to my friends.
3	Evan	Information Technology	I want to learn coding.
4	CJ	Plant Biology	Can I find wild edibles and write a booklet about how to find them and use them in a recipe?
5	Jesse	Great Pacific Garbage Patch	Will we ever be able to get rid of the plastic garbage in the ocean?
6	Rob	Construction	I want to build a cabinet for my room, so I need to make the design first.
7	Daeun	Art	I want to make a watercolor painting of my garden.
8	Jade	Sports and Math/Statistics	I want to compare college and major league baseball statistics to see if the best college players become the best professional players.

describe growth toward each target. Typically, each students' IBL plan includes a target related to each phase of the IBL process. As you see fit, this might also incorporate content, literacy, 21st-century, and/or social-emotional learning targets. For example, CJ's wild edibles project will naturally include all eight phases of the IBL process (meaning eight learning targets), but botany content and informative writing skills should probably also be included as learning targets (to say nothing about safety lessons related to collecting, identifying, and ingesting wild plants!).

We are aware of the time it would take to create eight or more learning targets for each of 10–25 different IBL projects in a classroom or school setting. In order to remedy this situation, we created two generic menus and a list of proficiency levels. The student-friendly proficiency levels are detailed in Resource 3. The first menu, Resource 4, lists each of the IBL phases, their learning targets, success criteria, and when the targets should be addressed. We anticipate that each learning target will be formatively assessed (and feedback provided) during these time periods. The second menu, Resource 5, includes the bulk of the standards-based targets for discipline content, literacy skills, 21st-century goals, and the SEL standards. This table also outlines learning targets, success criteria, and when the targets should be addressed.

Resource 4 and Resource 5 are also available as downloadable editable templates on the book's webpage. You can revise the wording as needed for your students or use only the targets and criteria relevant for a specific student's IBL project or for the timing of a given formative assessment conference. For example, Esteban's kitchen chemistry project might have 10 learning targets—one for each phase of the IBL process, another for the science content he will learn, and one to help him grow his communication skills. Alternatively, and depending on the nature of a student's IBL project, you and your students may create your own learning targets, proficiency levels, and criteria that do a better job aligning with the needs of the class and individual projects.

When this selection and revision process occurs, we recommend that students have the opportunity to work with their teachers to reword the targets, success criteria, and proficiency levels to support their own understanding and clarity. In fact, there is substantial research that supports the value of teaching students about the formative assessment process so that they understand the expectations and can eventually lead, or colead, the formative assessment review. These inclusionary actions provide yet another opportunity to promote student agency and self-management. For example, during the early stages of Jesse's project about the Great Pacific Ocean Garbage Patch, he suggested separating the resources and the research stages and making them two separate learning targets. He also wanted to delete experiments and design from the success criteria, and he thought that the resources should be measured at the beginning and middle of the project's lifespan.

Once the proficiency levels, targets, and criteria are selected, teachers and students decide on the evidence that will be used in tandem with the success criteria to measure growth toward the learning target. Evidence might include students' notes, resources, behaviors, paperwork, project drafts, and action plans. Such specific evidence is tied to a limited number of targets, further simplifying the management of the formative assessment process. For example, Jade quickly located the Society for American Baseball Research website and wanted to use her Chromebook e-notes as evidence of her research learning target and its success criteria.

All of these actions (i.e., deciding on the learning targets, selecting and revising the success criteria, and choosing the evidence of learning) precede decisions about the formative assessment format and schedule. The nature of formative assessment, and its effectiveness, assumes that such assessment happens more than once over

Name: _____ Date: _____

Student-Friendly Proficiency Levels

Proficiency Level	Evidence
Target	× I reached my target. × I know this because I can show proof for each of its success criteria.
Close to Target	× I am close to my target. × I know this because I can show proof for most of the criteria.
Halfway to Target	× I am halfway to my target. × I know this because I can show proof for half of the criteria.
Beginning Target	× I am beginning my project. × I know the target and the criteria. × I know what kind of project work to keep for measuring how close I am to the target. × I know how to measure this target.

RESOURCE 4

IBL Learning Targets and Success Criteria Menu

Directions: This menu was designed for teachers who want to use formative assessment to measure student proficiency with the various phases of the IBL process. The first column, "Learning Dimension," lists the various phases of the IBL process. The second column contains a student-friendly learning target for each phase, and the third column contains the criteria that can be used to measure the degree to which project work contains evidence of each criterion. The last column suggests the appropriate timing for the assessment of each target. Each learning target should be formatively assessed (and feedback provided) during these time periods.

Learning Dimension	Learning Target(s)	Student-Friendly Success Criteria	When to Address
Interest Finding	I can name my learning interests.	✗ I finished the whole survey. ✗ I added up my totals. ✗ I shared my survey results with other students and the teacher. ✗ I decided on an interesting topic for my project (even if it wasn't on the list).	Beginning of the project
Interest Focusing	I narrowed my interest into a project-sized topic.	✗ I can explain what I already know about my interest. ✗ I brainstormed different things I could do with my topic. ✗ I narrowed my interest to a manageable size. ✗ I have questions or ideas for new learning with my interest.	Beginning of the project
Goal Setting	I can name the goal for my project.	✗ My goal or question is interesting to me. ✗ I will have to do new learning to answer my question or reach my goal. ✗ My goal is doable. ✗ My goal is clear.	Beginning of the project

Learning Dimension	Learning Target(s)	Student-Friendly Success Criteria	When to Address
Action Planning	I made a plan for my project.	× My plan names my question or goal. × I made a timeline for the first few steps of my project. × I named some materials I will need. × I thought about how to share my learning.	Beginning of the project
Resources and Research	I can go on a hunt for the answers to my learning questions.	× I used books, the Internet, other people, observations, experimenting, and/or designing to answer my IBL questions. × The resources I used can be trusted. × I spent a lot of time investigating my learning questions × I made notes, drawings, or records of my research. × I organized all of my notes and records. × I decided what information was important and what wasn't important.	Middle of the project
Product	I can make a product that meets my goal.	× My product fits my goal or inquiry question. × You can see pieces of my new learning in the product. × I worked hard on the product. × My product is complete. × My product is polished.	End of the project
Communicating With an Audience	I had a discussion with other people about my project.	× I shared my new learning. × People understood my project. × People talked to me about my project.	End of the project

RESOURCE 5

Standards-Based Learning Targets and Success Criteria Menu

Directions: This menu was designed for teachers who want to use formative assessment to measure the content, literacy, 21st-century, and/or social-emotional learning standards that are aligned with each IBL project. The first column, "Learning Dimension," lists the various strands/categories of standards-based learning aligned with the IBL process. These dimensions are aligned with the fundamental expectations inherent in the standards. Special emphasis is placed on the 21st-century skills and the CCSS. The second column contains a student-friendly learning target for each strand, and the third column provides the criteria that can be used, along with appropriate project evidence, to measure growth toward the learning target. The last column suggests the appropriate timing for the assessment of each target. Each learning target should be formatively assessed (and feedback provided) during these time periods.

Learning Dimension	Learning Target(s)	Student-Friendly Success Criteria	When to Address
Project Content	I can name the questions that I answered for my project. I can name the new information I learned for my project.	× All of the answers to my questions are new learning for me. × I learned the answers to my questions. × I learned something new. × My new learning had some important ideas and results. × My learning made me have more questions.	Middle of the project, end of the project

Learning Dimension	Learning Target(s)	Student-Friendly Success Criteria	When to Address
Research	I can go on a hunt for the answers to my learning questions.	× I used books, the Internet, other people, observations, experimenting, and/or designing to answer my IBL questions. × The resources I used can be trusted. × I spent a lot of time investigating my learning questions × I made notes, drawings, or records of my research. × I organized all of my notes and records. × I decided what information was important.	Middle of the project, end of the project
Communication	I had a two-way talk with other people about my project.	× I shared my new learning. × People understood my project. × People talked to me about my project.	End of the project
Planning	I made a plan for my project.	× I made a plan before I started to work on my project. × I followed the plan. × I changed the plan when needed. × My plan was clear to me and other people. × I used the plan to focus my work.	Beginning of the project, middle of the project
Design	I can sketch or arrange the parts of my product, model, or design.	× I found a problem. × I collected information about the problem. × I brainstormed ideas. × I analyzed and reused some ideas. × I made a plan or a model. × My plan/model has details, steps, parts, and/or tasks. × I tested and improved my ideas. × My plans and models worked.	Middle of the project, end of the project

Learning Dimension	Learning Target(s)	Student-Friendly Success Criteria	When to Address
Reasoning	I can analyze my research notes and problems.	✕ I had to think hard to learn the answers to my question. ✕ I combined ideas from different places to get to my new idea. ✕ My new learning had some hard parts. ✕ My learning had some complicated parts.	Middle of the project, end of the project
Creativity	I can think of an original solution for my goal or problem.	✕ I started with my question or goal. ✕ I thought of lots of different ideas. ✕ I combined the best of my ideas. ✕ I evaluated my possible ideas. ✕ I made an action plan. ✕ I created my solution.	Middle of the project, end of the project
Communication	I shared my work with others.	✕ I talked about my project with people other than my teacher. ✕ I shared my work with people outside of my classroom. ✕ People understand my project. ✕ People talked with me about my project.	Middle of the project, end of the project
Collaboration	I used teamwork for part of my project.	✕ I worked with other people on some parts of my project. ✕ They helped me. ✕ I helped them. ✕ We shared ideas. ✕ We compromised. ✕ We worked together to finish parts of the project.	Middle of the project, end of the project
Problem Solving	I can tackle the problems in my project.	✕ I found a problem. ✕ I researched the cause and solution. ✕ I experimented with the solution. ✕ I judged my solution. ✕ I know what I need to do to try and fix things.	Middle of the project, end of the project

The Interest-Based Learning Coach © Prufrock Press Inc.

Learning Dimension	Learning Target(s)	Student-Friendly Success Criteria	When to Address
Agency	I can manage my project on my own.	× I am my own boss. × I made my own plan. × I made my own decisions. × I am in control of my project.	Middle of the project, end of the project
Self-Management	I can control my own feelings and actions.	× I stuck with my goal. × I didn't get distracted or waste time. × I persisted. × I was patient.	Middle of the project, end of the project

the course of a target's lifespan (the time between the initiation of a target and students' mastery of the target). This habitual multiplicity ensures that feedback is provided in time for students to deepen their understanding, address the unfinished aspects of the success criteria, and make needed improvements in the related work product.

However, the expectation for multiple formative assessment events over the life of each specific IBL project always abuts the reality of 11 or more individual and small-group IBL projects in a 25-student classroom. It also demands a practical plan for formative assessment. We recommend that a teacher use 30%–50% of the time allocated for each IBL session for formative assessment. This means that during a 90-minute IBL session, the teacher uses 30–45 minutes for some aspect of the formative assessment process. This time might be used to communicate or discuss targets, work with students to set criteria, assess student work, discuss feedback and next steps, or conduct feedback-related coaching and intervention. Resource 6 provides a visual representation of this process and its various components.

In order to conduct numerous formative assessments during each IBL session, each assessment needs to be brief and to the point. Although teachers can collect students' work folders and conduct formative assessment when students are not present, it is usually more beneficial, effective, and time-efficient to conduct the formative assessment while the student is in the classroom.

For this reason, we recommend the use of short 2- to 3-minute conferences, conversations, or observations as the formative assessment format for each small-group, partner, or individual IBL project. We also recommend that during any given formative assessment, only one or two targets are assessed. Resource 7 provides example scripts for teacher-led formative assessment conferences that can be accomplished in 3 minutes. The various purposes for a formative assessment conference are listed in the first column, and a sample script for beginning each type of conference is listed in the second column. The fourth and fifth categories, formative assessment and feedback, are typical of most formative assessment conferences.

Another way to shorten the formative assessment timeframe involves teaching and modeling the formative assessment process for students. Teachers can encourage students to prepare for the conversation or conference by scheduling their conference in advance, notifying them, and asking them to bring the appropriate evidence of learning with them to the conference.

For teachers who are interested in encouraging students to lead the formative assessment and feedback process themselves, we have also included a quick start guide for student use (see Resource 8). This approach encourages both agency and ownership of the learning process. If students use this reference guide prior to a scheduled formative assessment conversation or conference, they are more likely to have located and organized the relevant evidence of learning prior to the start of the conversation. This card also jumpstarts their thinking and encourages students

Quick Start Card for Student-Led Formative Assessment and Feedback Conferences

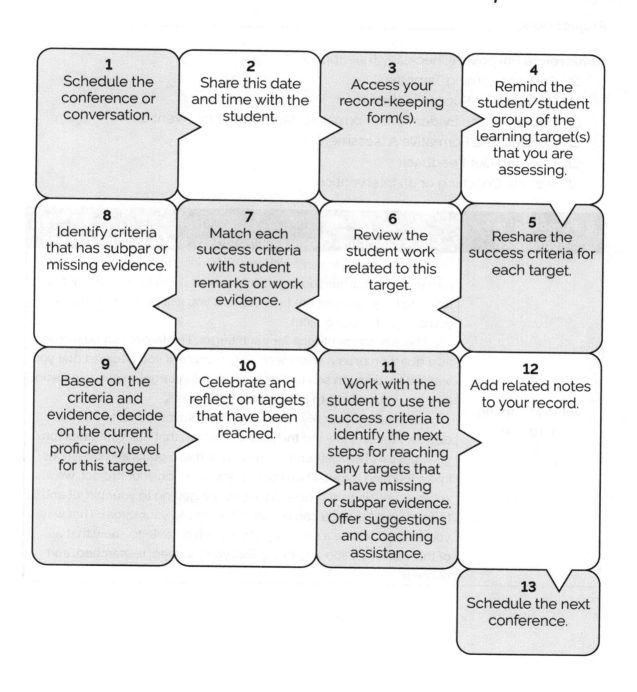

1 Schedule the conference or conversation.

2 Share this date and time with the student.

3 Access your record-keeping form(s).

4 Remind the student/student group of the learning target(s) that you are assessing.

8 Identify criteria that has subpar or missing evidence.

7 Match each success criteria with student remarks or work evidence.

6 Review the student work related to this target.

5 Reshare the success criteria for each target.

9 Based on the criteria and evidence, decide on the current proficiency level for this target.

10 Celebrate and reflect on targets that have been reached.

11 Work with the student to use the success criteria to identify the next steps for reaching any targets that have missing or subpar evidence. Offer suggestions and coaching assistance.

12 Add related notes to your record.

13 Schedule the next conference.

RESOURCE 7 ━━━━━━

Conference Categories and Conversation Scripts

Project Goal: _____

Conference Purpose: (Check any that apply.)
- ❑ Set the Learning Target(s)
- ❑ Develop the Success Criteria
- ❑ Decide on the Evidence for Formative Assessment Intervention
- ❑ Conduct the Formative Assessment
- ❑ Give and Get Feedback
- ❑ Provide Coaching or an Intervention

Purpose of the Conference	Script Examples, Conversation Starters, and Guiding Questions
Set the Learning Target(s)	"We are going to have a short conference today so that we can turn your project question/goal into one or more learning targets. A learning target names the learning that you will be able to show after you complete your project. There is one sentence for each target. The target can be worded as a question or as a statement. For example, if you decided that you wanted to research sea turtles, your learning target might say, 'I want to learn how I can help protect sea turtle nests.' Let's look at your My Action Plan (see Resource 12) to help us decide. Please show me the part of the plan that has your question/goal. Let's work together to turn each of these goals and questions into a learning target. Then later, as you work on your project, we will meet again to see how close you are getting to your target and to figure out how you can get all of the way to your target. That way your project will be a success, and we will be able to show that all of this work was about learning that you planned, researched, and finished."

RESOURCE 7, CONTINUED

Purpose of the Conference	Script Examples, Conversation Starters, and Guiding Questions
Develop the Success Criteria	"We are going to have a short conference today so that we can decide how we want to measure your project work to see how close it keeps getting to your learning target(s). We will use criteria to make these measurements. Criteria describe the characteristics we expect to see in a project that hits the learning target. I am going to show you a set of criteria that I think match your project and your learning target. I'd like you to help me decide if they match your thinking. When we decide, we will use your learning target, these criteria, and your project work as yardsticks to measure how close your work is to the target."
Decide on the Evidence for Formative Assessment Intervention	"During your project about _____, you and I will have a few chances to talk about how your work is going, how close you are getting to your goal, and if you need any help. We will use your project work and the learning criteria we already spoke about as our mile markers to measure how far along you are toward your journey to your project goal. Right now, let's look more closely at your project plans to find out what work we can look at to see your mile markers. Let's try to make a match between each criterion and your project work. Where in your project work do you think we will see your first criterion, your second, etc.? Great work. Now when we meet to discuss your project progress we will use this project work to measure your learning targets."
Conduct the Formative Assessment	Recall the target, criteria, and evidence. Find the criteria in the evidence, decide on the level of the criteria. Is the gas tank half full, empty, or full?
Give and Get Feedback	"Over the last few minutes, we have had a chance to look closely at your learning target, its measurement criteria, and your evidence. We found that the project work met a few/some/most/all of the criteria. Let's focus on the criteria that still need some work. What might we do to show that criteria in your project work? What is the next step for this project target?"
Provide Coaching or an Intervention	"During our last conference, we made a plan that would get your project to match criteria _____. We decided that _____ would be the next step for the project. We are here today so that I can help you with that plan and its next step. Let's get started!"

RESOURCE 8

Quick Start Card for Student-Led Formative Assessment and Feedback Conferences

1

Before the Conference:
- Know when your target review is scheduled.
- Before the conference, think about your target, success criteria, and evidence.
- What is the target that you are going to measure?
- Look at the target's success criteria. Which ones are in your work? Decide what evidence you need to bring to the conference to show the criteria.
- Look at the target levels. How close are you to the target?
- Bring your evidence to the conference.

2

During the Conference:
- Retell your target.
- Retell the success criteria.
- Show the teacher where the evidence touches on each criterion.
- Together, use the levels to decide how close you are to the target.
- Together, decide on the next steps you need to do to reach the target.

3

After the Conference:
- Remember your feedback decisions.
- Get any help or materials you need.
- Work on the incomplete target criteria.
- Make sure to work on every criterion that wasn't complete.
- When all of the criteria are strong, gather the evidence that shows the improvements.
- Tell the teacher you would like to schedule a follow-up conference.

to develop questions, remarks, or responses about the target, criteria, and evidence. Some students, like Jade, may even begin the conference by saying, "I already did my own target grading!"

Unless teachers are blessed with a remarkable long-term memory, they also need a place to record notes about each student's formative assessment results and related feedback suggestions. The Excel spreadsheet or Google Sheets format we described earlier in this chapter provides one method for record keeping. Yet another method is to record each conference on a separate form similar to Resource 9: Formative Assessment Conference Record Form. This format can also be digital and organized into folders, one for each student. The form includes comprehensive directions, a complete proficiency level description, and a place to record codes or short notes about each target and their criteria, evidence, proficiency level, and feedback. An editable version is available on the book's webpage.

The last aspect of formative assessment, regardless of the phase of the IBL process, is to provide the follow-up coaching, resources, redirection, or intervention specified in the target's feedback. This opportunity for support and revision is the most important aspect of formative assessment. It "seals the deal" and ensures that formative assessment does what it was intended to do; it provides the just-in-time attention that supports target mastery for all students.

Conclusion

Many curriculum and assessment specialists suggest that there should be strong linkages between any learning opportunity, its goals, and its assessment. The same is true for IBL. All of our students' design, exploration, research, and service work should have measurable targets. Ideally, these targets should be specific to each student's interests, prior knowledge, and plans. Practicality suggests that each student's project targets should be achievable and easily measured with readily available evidence, succinct and student-friendly success criteria, and time allocations that are realistic and demonstrate equity for all students in the class.

This chapter provided information about the definition, role, and benefits of formative assessment within an IBL initiative, including specific templates, options, and steps for using formative assessment across the numerous phases of an IBL project. This chapter concludes the discussion of the background and foundational information that supports interest-based learning. We have explained how this book is organized, analyzed the components of the IBL framework, and discussed how to form a shared vision for IBL and provide for its sound foundation. In the next chapter, we begin a discussion of the eight phases of the IBL process.

RESOURCE 9

Formative Assessment Conference Record Form

Directions:

1. Revise this form as needed.

2. Prepare a print or an electronic copy of this form for each conference.

3. Schedule student conferences for 1–5 minutes each.

4. In advance, tell students the date, time, and purpose of their assessment conference.

5. Ask students to bring My Action Plan (see Resource 12) and their project work to the conference.

6. Assess only 1–3 criteria per conference.

7. Copy and paste the learning targets and the success criteria from the student's MAP as well as the other SEL, content literacy, and content standards' criteria that the teacher wants to assess.

8. Use the "warm-up" questions to establish a collaborative and respectful climate.

9. Remind students of the purpose of the conference.

10. Ask students to lead the conference by asking and answering the guiding questions while you listen, take notes, and sometimes ask clarifying questions.

11. Give students a copy of the proficiency levels. If necessary, help them find their project's learning targets and success criteria.

12. Ask students (or help students) to measure each target using the criteria and the evidence they brought to the conference.

13. Working with the student, identify the current proficiency level for each target.

14. Together, decide on the next steps for moving closer to the target. Offer help as needed. Note the feedback plan on the conference form.

Warm-Up and Guiding Questions	
× How is your project coming along? What are you enjoying? What are you working on right now? Can you tell me why we are meeting today?	× What criteria are we using to measure the target?
× What is the target we are measuring at this conference?	× Measure the evidence with the target and its criteria. How would you rate it?
× What evidence or work are we using to measure the target?	× How can I help you reach your target?
× What is the next step for moving closer to the target?	

Proficiency Level	Evidence
Target	× I reached my target. × I know this because I can show proof for each of its success criteria.
Close to Target	× I am close to my target. × I know this because I can show proof for most of the criteria.
Halfway to Target	× I am halfway to my target. × I know this because I can show proof for half of the criteria.
Beginning Target	× I am beginning my project. × I know the target and the criteria. × I know what kind of project work to keep for measuring how close I am to the target. × I know how to measure this target.

Student's Name: _____

IBL Project: _____

Conference Date: _____

Project Status: _____

Target	Criteria	Evidence	Proficiency Level	Feedback

Notes:

CHAPTER 5

Finding Interests

I think the big mistake in schools is trying to teach children anything, and by using fear as the basic motivation. Fear of getting failing grades, fear of not staying with your class, etc. Interest can produce learning on a scale compared to fear as a nuclear explosion to a firecracker.

—Stanley Kubrick

At this point, you have invited and "hooked" students into IBL, as well as established a common classroom culture for the work. What's next? We start with students' interests, Step 1 in the IBL process. "But I have so many students!" you exclaim. "How am I supposed to figure out what interests each of my students? It's impossible!" It's not really impossible, we say. One just has to be systematic and planful. We have an interest survey for you to use, ideas for how to showcase the interests for the entire class to see and use, and step-by-step procedures for conducting student conferences and record keeping.

After reading this chapter, you will be able to:

1. explain the connection among interests, motivation, and learning;
2. use an interest survey to identify each student's top two interest topics and clusters;
3. identify two ways to utilize students' interests during regular classroom instruction;

4. conference with students to determine their interest topics; and
5. keep accurate and efficient records of student conferences.

You may want to read the case studies about Jared and Fatima either before reading or after reading this chapter. These cases in Appendix A profile young people who needed additional support to uncover an interest area.

Connections Between Interests, Motivation, and Learning

What are student interests? This might seem like a silly, simple question, but it is deceptively simple. We provided a brief definition of an interest in Chapter 1. Now we want to look more closely at how interests develop, strengthen, and propel one across a life span. Educators often take for granted that they know what student interests are. Equally important, educators recognize that student interests are usually so low on their teaching radar, with so many other things to do, that teachers often overlook them.

Recent literature suggests that student interests need a more prominent role in the classroom. Student interests (1) are developed, not innate; (2) can be both a psychological state of attention and affect toward an object or topic; (3) are malleable and can—with nurturing—become an enduring and stable predisposition to reengage over time; (4) can be promoted using a four-phase model that guides the development of new interest and capitalizes on existing interests (Harackiewicz et al., 2008); and (5) can predict traditional measures of student success, including future course-taking patterns and performance.

"Yikes," you exclaim! "I have spent so much time on district and federal initiatives like the Every Student Succeeds Act and No Child Left Behind, and trying to increase my students' performance levels that I have unwittingly overlooked a HUGE opportunity to find and sustain my students' interests, perhaps a key to their motivation and performance." Not to worry! We're about to remedy that scenario.

In Appendix B, we discuss the connection among the three theories that underpin our work here: social development theory (Vygotsky, 1978), self-determination theory (Deci & Ryan, 1985), and the theory of optimal learning environments (Csikszentmihalyi, 1990). Specifically, we talk about the connection among the three theories as they relate to classroom choice, learning, and motivation. We state:

> With these understandings as a backdrop, we propose that these three theories can be considered one formula for student success. If

choice can get students into a state of flow and their ZPD, you can increase their intrinsic motivation. Likewise, if—through choice— you can increase students' motivation and self-determination, you may be able to increase students' time on task, the overall quality of their work, and, hopefully, their long-term learning and feelings of accomplishment, efficacy, and agency.

What happens if we add a verifiable and genuine student interest into the "formula for student success" we have articulated? That is, what happens when you provide students with a choice about which of their top, genuine interests they would like to pursue in the classroom? Our field experiences suggest a multiplier effect. We believe that if practitioners are able to couple educational choice with a student's interest area(s), powerful results will emerge. Hidi and Renninger (2006) reported, "The level of a person's interest has repeatedly been found to be a powerful influence on learning. Specifically, interest has been found to influence: attention, goals, and levels of learning" (p. 111). Quite simply, we have seen some of our most reluctant learners move into hyperdrive.

> I like developing my own topics because I get to work on things that I am really interested in. I think I work harder and longer.
>
> **—PEDRO, GRADE 4**

Tomlinson and Jarvis (2006) wrote eloquently on this issue: "When the manual doesn't fit the learner, stop studying the how-to list and start studying your students." They go on to say: "It's not a matter of either teaching the curriculum or teaching students. Good teaching is inevitably the fine art of connecting content and kids—of doing what it takes to adapt how we teach so that what we teach takes hold in the lives and minds of students" (p. 16). Let's be real now so that we are not accused of using hyperbole. Capitalizing on students' interests is *not* a silver bullet for student motivation, sustained interest, and learning. It is, however, one more robust technique that we can add to our repertoire of strategies for student success. Think of it as a different, yet potent, way to approach student learning.

Collecting Information on Your Students' Interests

The web is replete with thousands of interest surveys for practitioners. In fact, our most recent web search retrieved 11,500 hits in .55 seconds. So many choices and not enough time! If you want to cull through the resources, there are plenty online. For those of you who may not have the luxury of all of that extra time, we provide you with an interest survey (see Appendix C). We designed the survey with several thoughts in mind. First, we designed two versions: one for lower elementary (grades K–4) and the other for upper elementary and middle school (grades 5–8). The former is shorter and includes more easily recognizable words. With that said, kindergarteners and lower elementary grade students may yet need some support to complete the early grades version. Second, we state openly and up front that we could not include every interest topic that young people might have. (So little space for the infinite list of topics students might find interesting!) Thus, we designed an editable version of the survey so that you can customize it for the unique needs of your students (see the book's webpage). Third, we used the National Career Clusters Framework to organize our potential interest topics (Advance CTE, n.d.). The 16 career clusters represent a distinct grouping of occupations and industries.

To ensure that young people are able to readily grasp the meaning of the abstract nature of each of the 16 career cluster names, we created Table 4. The left-hand column contains the original name of the career cluster. The middle column and right-hand column contain simplified names for middle school students and younger elementary students, respectively. Note that the simplified wording is repeated on the different forms of the interest survey (see Appendix C). Note also that we added two additional areas of student interest.

Fourth, and finally, if you use the interest survey at regular intervals, you will be able to note trends and patterns with a particular student's interests or across students' interests. For example, if a student's interests occur in the tourism cluster repeatedly, the child may pursue a vocation in that area. If you work with your students to develop their talents, we hope this tool will prove invaluable.

"I love gymnastics! I take classes on Saturdays and everything."

—SHELLY, KINDERGARTEN

TABLE 4

Career Clusters Crosswalk for Interest Inventories

Career Cluster	Suggested Title, Grades 5–8	Suggested Title, Grades K–4
Agriculture, Food & Natural Resources	Farming, Food, and Resources	Plants, Food, and Resources
Architecture & Construction	Architecture and Buildings	Buildings
Arts, A/V Technology & Communications	Art, Media, Music, Technology, and Communication	Art, Music, and Communication
Business Management & Administration	Business and Bosses	Business and Bosses
Education & Training	Teaching in School and Business	Teaching Others
Finance	Budgets, Banks, and Money	Banks, Money, Budgets, and Keeping Records
Government & Public Administration	Government	Rules, Helping Others
Health Science	Health and Wellness	Helping Sick People and Animals; Staying Healthy
Hospitality & Tourism	Tourism	New Places, People, and Cultures
Human Services	Helping Services and People	Caring About People and Their Problems, Volunteering
Information Technology	Computer Technology	Computers
Law, Public Safety, Corrections & Security	Law, Safety, and Security	Protecting People; Safety, Laws, Debate, and Making Arguments
Marketing	Buying and Selling	Buying and Selling Products and Services
Manufacturing	Factories and Designing and Making Products	Machines, Repair, Design, Tools, Equipment

TABLE 4, CONTINUED

Career Cluster	Suggested Title, Grades 5–8	Suggested Title, Grades K–4
Science, Technology, Engineering & Mathematics	STEM	Science, Math, Inventing, and Building
Transportation, Distribution & Logistics	Moving People and Things Now and in the Future	Trucks, Boats, Planes, and Trains
Fashion*	Fashion	Clothes Design, Fashion Design
Sports and Recreation*	Sports	Games, Teams, Sports, Play, and Recreation

Note. Career clusters are listed from the National Career Clusters Framework (Advance CTE, n.d.). The clusters marked with an asterisk (*) are additions because they are long-standing areas of interest for students.

Now that you have reviewed the instrument and decided how you will administer it, use the following talking points with students as you prepare to identify their interests for your IBL initiative. You can, of course, prepare your own list of comments.

- × As we begin our IBL projects, we will need to know your interests.
- × Everyone has many potential interest areas.
- × Interests can be nurtured and developed.
- × Once we know what your interests are, we will focus on one or two of them to begin your project work.
- × There are many tools we can use to identify our potential areas of interest: journals, conversations, your responses to things that we do in class, for example.
- × We have chosen to use _____ as our interest survey tool. It should take you about 25–30 minutes to complete.

While students are completing the My Interests Survey (see Appendix C), distribute two sticky notes to each student. Once students have completed the survey, ask them to rank their top two career clusters and interest topics. Then, invite them to (1) write them both on the lines provided at the end of the My Interests Survey and (2) write one interest on each sticky note. Ask students to put the sticky notes aside for the next activity, explained in the following section. When students have completed the survey, as well as their two sticky notes, collect the surveys.

Showcasing Your Interest Data in the Classroom

How can you use your students' interest information? You must collect and organize students' interest surveys. Paper copies and/or digital copies need to be filed and stored away so that they can be referenced during the individual and small-group conferences that will be part of the interest focusing discussions, the next step in the IBL process. Students' interest information can also be used to inform classroom instruction in many ways, and we are delighted to suggest a technique that has proved successful in our classrooms.

My Interests Mural and Gallery Walk

Explain to your students that you are keeping their completed surveys to support the interest focusing activity that you will conduct with them individually or in small groups in the next week or so. At that time, you will dialogue with each of them to focus their interests into one or two inquiry questions that they can investigate during the allotted weekly class time during IBL.

In the meantime, share with students that there are other ways that you want to tap into their interests. One way to do so is to create a class mural of their sticky notes. Point out the wall space/mural/bulletin board that you have prepared for this activity. It doesn't make any difference where they post their sticky notes, as long as they are within the allotted space.

Then, and in small groups, invite class members to position their sticky notes on the designated space. Once all students have posted their sticky notes, invite students to complete a gallery walk of the notes. Their task, during the gallery walk, is to answer the following question: What trends and patterns do you notice about the posted notes?

When the class has completed the gallery walk, invite small groups (3–5 students) to compare notes. Follow this activity with a whole-class debriefing. Our field trials suggest that students will likely observe any of the following, for example:
- the similarities among the interests,
- the differences among the interests,
- the diversity of class interests, and
- that some students, based on similar interests, might like to work together on their IBL project.

Share with students that you plan to use this mural not only as you proceed with your IBL plans, but also in your regular classroom instruction. Further, you can suggest that students:

×   graph the data,
×   chart class interests over time to see how they change, and
×   classify the sticky notes by career clusters to predict possible occupations of class members.

Share with students that you also plan to incorporate student interests into your instruction in at least two ways. First, you will try to reference their interests at least once a day. Second, you will try to incorporate their interests in some way in daily/weekly lessons. Once you have utilized a sticky note, remove it from the mural. In this way, you will be able to use as many of the students' interests as possible.

Conducting Your Interest Interviews Based on the My Interests Survey

Your next questions will probably be: "Well, now what do I do when I interview my students? How do I prepare students? How do I schedule them? What do I say during the conference? How can I keep track of all of this information?" As you might remember, we talked about conferencing with students in Chapter 2. Our goal here is to (1) elaborate on those early words and (2) answer the questions that might now be going around in your head as your first set of conferences approaches.

Before we suggest some easy steps that you could follow, note that we call these conferences *reflective conferences*. They are slightly different from other conferences that you read about in Chapter 4, when you read about check-in, coaching, and formative assessment conferences. In a reflective conference, you will spend time with individual or small groups of students thinking, asking probing questions based upon their input, and reflecting back to them what you hear. Your goal, in this case, is to help students better understand exactly what truly interests them about a particular topic. Sometimes it's easy to listen up front, get an idea of where you think a student wants to go, and then channel the rest of the conference in that direction. That teacher-directedness, however, is not the goal of an IBL conference. The real goal is to listen intently to uncover exactly what makes students passionate about the topic, reflect those thoughts back to the students, and enable their realization of the idea. All the while, you are modeling for students the metacognition that they can adopt to become more independent thinkers and engaged learners. It's a win-win.

Step 1: Preparing Students for Conferences

Share the following with students:

Now that you have completed the My Interests Survey, I want to work individually with you to learn more about your starting points for an IBL initiative. I will be scheduling each of you for a conference that is about 5 minutes long, and we will work together to talk about your interest areas. I will put the names of students with whom I will conference on the board each day with a time slot. When it's your turn, you can come up to my table/desk.

So that we can work best together, please be thinking about what specifically interests you about the topic(s) you have listed on your survey. When I give you your conference time, please bring your thoughts with you. Our goal is to target one specific interest area for your IBL project. Don't worry if you do not have any detailed thoughts about your interest area when you visit with me. We will work through it together.

Step 2: Scheduling Student Conferences

We believe that most of your student conferences should take about 5–6 minutes. Surely, you will be able to conduct student conferences during the weekly time that you are designating for your IBL. Within a 45-minute segment of class time (90 minutes if you have a block schedule), you should be able to conduct at least nine to 10 meetings. Additionally, our field experiences suggest that you can capture minutes during class time that are not designated to IBL. With that in mind, as well as estimating that you have 20–25 students, we believe that you will be able to meet with each student within a 2-week window. Many of you will be able to accomplish the meetings in less time than we propose.

Step 3: Preparing for Conferences

To make the best use of your conference time, you should briefly review students' interest surveys so that you have a general idea of their two top interests. Don't think too much about a student's or small groups of students' interests. Be careful that you do not become so invested in the interest area that you subsequently take over the upcoming conference and end up telling the student(s) a specific topic in the targeted area and negate your role as a collaborator and reflector of student thinking.

Step 4: Conducting Conferences

We usually begin a conference with a question. In this case, you will probably start by asking each student, "What were your top interests?" More than likely, you will need to listen intently to a student's answers. If a student says, sports, for example, you know that response is too general. Thus, you will next want to ask probing questions, such as "What about sports interests you?" "Is there a sport that is most interesting to you?" "Is it watching sports that you like . . . the rules of the game . . . the players?"

Your dialogue should continue until you can comfortably say something like the following: "I think I hear you saying that you like professional football. Is that right?" If the student agrees, then additional probing questions might be in order. After those questions and answers, you might refine the interest area by saying, "And further, do I hear you saying that you like the Patriots and the Packers? Do I have that right?" Support students to write down their interest areas on the My Interests Survey if they have not already done so.

"I've always been given and assigned topics that have been created by teachers . . . and I feel obligated to write about a topic that is SO disinteresting. No kidding! . . . [This] seriously affects the quality of my work."

—ZABI, GRADE 8

Continue with the conference in the same reflective, back-and-forth manner to identify specific topics for students' second top interest area. Finally, thank each student for their good thinking, and share that they should keep their My Interests Survey in their IBL folder (if applicable). Explain that the thinking they did with you will help to guide their upcoming work, especially in the next conference in which you will both work to develop an inquiry question around each of the two topics.

Step 5: Recording Your Findings

Although recording your findings will most likely be the last thing you do in a conference, it is one of your most important tasks. Make sure that you spend enough time at the end of each conference or the end of the day to update students' folders with notes about your conference outcomes. Be as timely as you can with the data recording after student conferences. We know from experience that the process will be much easier and enjoyable if you plan ahead for organizing all of the information related to each student.

In Chapter 7, we provide a template called Project Tracker (see p. 106). It is designed expressly for teacher record-keeping in an IBL initiative, and it contains a specific place to record a student's two top interests. You may wish to reference it now to see how you might begin using it for efficient and effective record-keeping.

As practitioners, we have kept both paper copies of notes, as well as electronic formats. If you decide on paper copies, plan a notebook, at least 3 inches wide with 25–30 tab separators. If it makes things easier, use numbers for each student. For example, Elaine might be number 4. In the front of the binder, you can always keep a key page on which you have a roster of your students' names and assigned number. This way, you can easily flip to any student's information efficiently. If you decide to go electronically, set up an umbrella folder for your IBL initiative. Inside the larger folder, you can make individual student folders. You can further subdivide each students' folder into as many categories or files as you wish, depending upon how you like to organize and track student information.

We hope that the steps listed and explained in this chapter will prove helpful. If you have your own way of conducting reflective conferences, no worries! You may already have a preferred method of securing the requisite information necessary for a successful IBL initiative.

Conclusion

You should now be comfortable (1) explaining the connection among interests, motivation, and learning; (2) using and administering some version of a self-selected interest inventory; (3) finding at least two other ways to incorporate student interests into the regular classroom beyond the IBL initiative (and thereby honoring your students and your relationship with them); (4) conducting the first round of reflective conferences to identify specific topics in students' interest areas; and (5) recording indispensable information about each student's IBL project.

In the next chapter, you will build upon your work to identify students' interests. you will explore how to take each student's top interest topic and rework it into an inquiry question, Step 3 of the IBL process.

CHAPTER 6

Focusing Interests

> Contrary to what we usually believe, moments like these, the best moments in our lives, are not the passive, receptive, relaxing times—although such experiences can also be enjoyable, if we have worked hard to attain them. The best moments usually occur when a person's body or mind is stretched to its limits in a voluntary effort to accomplish something difficult and worthwhile. . . . For each person there are thousands of opportunities, challenges to expand ourselves. (Csikszentmihalyi, 1990, p. 4)

At this point, you have identified at least one interest topic for each of your students and, perhaps, one or two of their top-ranking career clusters. We hope that your conferences about their interests provided you with validation regarding your hunches about some students' interest topics, at least a few pleasant surprises, and some "aha" experiences. With that done, you have completed Step 1 in the IBL process.

Now, you are on to Step 2, interest focusing. Once you have a general idea of a student's interest area, the next step is to rework it into a specific, researchable, inquiry question. To do so, you will be engaging in a large-group discussion with students followed by a reflective conference, once again, with individual and small groups of students. The intent of both the large-group instruction and the second round of conferencing is to guide students as they transform their interest area into an important and burning inquiry question. This inquiry question becomes one of the "thousands of opportunities" Csikszentmihalyi (1990) alluded to in the quotation that opens this chapter. The customized inquiry questions that students will generate become the launching pad for each student to expand themselves.

After reading this chapter, you will be able to:

1. understand the nature of inquiry and inquiry questions;
2. outline possible real-world problem areas related to students' interest areas;
3. conduct reflective conferences with individual and small groups of students to support their thinking as they transform or rework topics into a customized, high-quality inquiry question; and
4. help students assess the overall quality of their inquiry question.

You may want to read the case study about Tiffany, Aliyah, Kinzey, Katherine, and Alison either before reading or after reading this chapter (see Appendix A). This case study profiles a small group of students who work diligently, with teacher guidance, to focus a topic they could all agree upon.

What Is Inquiry?

Many might think that inquiry is exclusive to science. Actually, it is an approach to learning that cuts across disciples. It refers to a dynamic, interactive process that occurs between a student and knowledge. It begins when students are open to wonder and puzzlement and, through a systematic investigation of a targeted inquiry question, come to know and understand the world more clearly. Students' curiosity, wonder, and/or interest lead to asking an inquiry question, making discoveries, and testing those discoveries in a search for new understanding. Learners must find their own pathway through this process. Unlike learning in the classroom, which is traditionally linear, inquiry learning is a series of events, cyclical and iterative, because it is driven by the need for knowledge. Ultimately, learners must make meaning or sense from their experiences and resources, including books, exhibits, the insights of others, field events, and videos, to name a few. Through reflection, conversations with others, the interpretation of data, and observations, student researchers develop new knowledge to answer to their initial inquiry question.

In the 21st century, inquiry is a critical educational goal. Schools must shift their emphasis from "what we know" to "how we come to know." We believe that IBL is a perfect, responsible, and exciting choice for preparing students for the 21st century. We also believe that students learn more deeply, efficiently, and quickly if they sense that they have a real purpose for learning. This intentionality and purposeful solution finding is at the heart of inquiry; it extends our possibilities as teachers and students. As such, it is a profoundly fulfilling experience.

Why Use an Inquiry Question Rather Than a Topic?

Imagine being a student once again. How often do you hear the word *topic*? Your days are replete with assignments about topics: book report topics; fine arts studies around topics such as composers or artists, landscapes, movement, etc.; social studies topics and projects; science investigations and experiments about current topics; and language arts units about topics and themes. "So," you ask, "Why not just give a topic to students for their IBL project? They are used to the idea already!"

There are at least three reasons we encourage practitioners to help students refine their interest area into a research question rather than a topic:

×   Topics are often too broad, too abstract, and too general. In our collective experiences, topics are often so broad, in fact, that students cannot articulate what they are trying to accomplish.

×   Topics, once research is underway, often splinter into many subtopics, thereby leaving the student inquirer wondering what direction to pursue.

×   Topics, because they are too general, often lead students to write a report about a topic rather than to answer a specific question about the topic. And reports are *not* the objective of IBL initiatives; self-directed research that focuses squarely on an inquiry question and generates new information for the student is the goal.

Developing Inquiry Questions

How do you support the development of high-quality, student-driven inquiry questions? We believe it takes at least four steps: webbing the targeted interest area; analyzing and uncovering possible real-world avenues for the interest area through conferencing; drafting an initial, student-driven inquiry question; and finally, assessing the overall quality of the question and making any refinements. Each step is explained here in sequence and with examples.

Step 1: Webbing Students' Targeted Interest Areas

Webbing is a technique that makes thinking visual. It involves creating a web, a visual map that shows how different categories of information relate to one another.

One begins at the center oval or bubble with a keyword. During IBL, this keyword should be one of a student's top interests. It will be connected to other ovals around the center word. The bubbles around the center bubble contain real-world topics/ideas related to the interest area and can be used to jumpstart thinking about a problem that a student might investigate. See Resource 10: Web Template. This simple tool and brainstorming method will provide structure for ideas and facts, thereby creating a flexible framework for idea development, organizing, prioritizing, and decision making. You can use this tool and technique to support your conversations with individual and small groups of students to identify possible real-world problems and projects that appeal to their interest areas.

Another option is software we use, called Inspiration, to complete students' focusing activities. It is available in two age brackets. Kidspiration is a desktop package for students ages 4–9. Inspiration 9 is a desktop package designed for students ages 8 and up. The same company also offers a web-based package that lives on the cloud and can be accessed from anywhere with Internet. Inspiration offers free 30-day trials for each software package, and multiple packages are available in a tiered pricing structure. There are also other webbing software packages available, such as Bubbl.us and Lucidchart. Should you prefer these, information about each is available readily through an online search.

When you decide how you will have students web their interests, you are almost ready to start your next round of student conferences. Before you start organizing and conducting them, however, you might want to complete a sample webbing activity with the whole class as guided practice. The guided practice will give students a preview of what to expect when they meet individually or in small groups with you. To complete this guided practice, you will need about 30-40 minutes, to display Resource 10 or a drawn version of the web, and some background information about a topic. To assist you, we created a completed web about graffiti (see Figure 3).

If you so choose, you can use the following process to facilitate your guided practice.

1. Enter the targeted interest into the center oval.
2. Ask students: "What might be the first step you could take to determine how to turn an interest area into an inquiry question . . . something you are passionate about for an IBL project?"
3. If they do not know, you can share: "You might have to do a little more research or investigation."
4. Share with students that they can find more information either in a book about the topic or online.
5. Demonstrate what you mean, either with the book from the library or an online search about your identified topic. With regard to the book, show students the table of contents or index, and demonstrate how you can

RESOURCE 10
Web Template

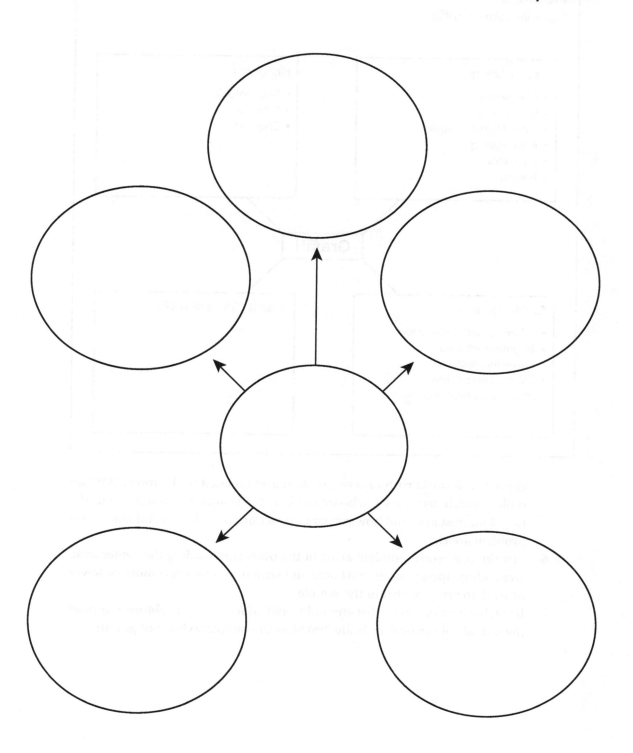

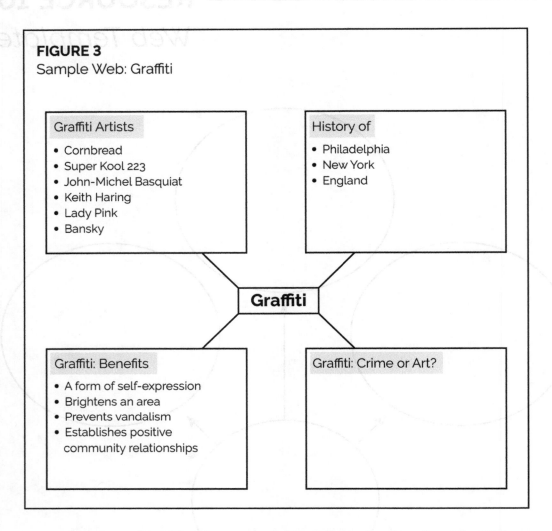

FIGURE 3
Sample Web: Graffiti

Graffiti Artists

- Cornbread
- Super Kool 223
- John-Michel Basquiat
- Keith Haring
- Lady Pink
- Bansky

History of

- Philadelphia
- New York
- England

Graffiti

Graffiti: Benefits

- A form of self-expression
- Brightens an area
- Prevents vandalism
- Establishes positive community relationships

Graffiti: Crime or Art?

extract real-world pathways or problem areas related to the topic. With an online search, use the whiteboard to show the results of a search about the target interest area and how you can extract many pathways and real-world problem areas.

6. List the real-world problem areas in the ovals surrounding the center oval. Depending upon your interest area and search, you may use more or fewer ovals than are provided in the sample.

7. If you have time, you can list any additional information or subtopics around the outside of the oval, as is illustrated in the sample web about graffiti.

Step 2: Targeting Real-World Subtopics Related to the Interest Area

Invite students to imagine that graffiti is their interest area. In a think-pair-share, invite students to talk about the possibilities you generated and decide on which pathways they would elect to pursue. For example, students might elect to examine the history of graffiti, research noted artists in the field, explore whether graffiti is an art form or defacement of public property, and/or explore graffiti across time periods or cultures. Afterward, debrief the entire class so that students can see the multiple real-world subtopics that can spin off an interest topic.

Step 3: Reworking the Subtopic Into an Inquiry Question

In another round of think-pair-share, ask students to list two to three specific questions that might interest them for the real-world area they identified. Have students share their questions with the class. Showcase for students the many and varied inquiry questions that emerge. Examples include, but are not limited to:

- × What is the history of graffiti?
- × What are the purposes of graffiti?
- × How has graffiti changed over time?
- × Does graffiti exist across cultures, and, if so, what are some common threads? Are there differences among cultures with respect to graffiti?
- × Is graffiti an art form or mindless vandalism?
- × In what ways does graffiti inform social protest, or does social protest inform graffiti?

Debrief as a class about students' question generation. What was hard? What was easy? How did they use the subtopics or pathways to generate a potential inquiry question?

Step 4: Assessing the Merit of Inquiry Questions

Share with students that good inquiry questions share some traits in common. (See Figure 4 for examples of good inquiry questions, as well as Figure 5 for some that need to be reworked.) Students can use the traits to help determine whether they have created an inquiry question that is powerful enough to guide their upcoming IBL project. A good inquiry question:

FIGURE 4

Examples of High-Quality Inquiry Questions

1. What traits do billionaires possess that make them so successful?
2. What makes for a great playground?
3. What do fictional villains in American literature tell us about American values?
4. What are the most sustainable farming methods?
5. How does my community recycle plastics?
6. What makes a social movement successful?
7. What rights should the accused have?
8. How can we predict traffic jams?
9. What is the most effective and efficient way to design an airport for a large metropolitan area?
10. How can we use water/energy in more sustainable ways?
11. How do different 4-H judges rate farm animals (e.g., sheep, ponies, milk cows) to ensure equity?

× lacks a full answer, has not already been answered, has not been answered completely, or has not been answered for the student's specific context;
× is clear;
× is focused;
× is open-ended;
× raises additional questions and jumpstarts further inquiry;
× reflects a true and abiding interest of the student;
× is manageable within the timeframe of IBL in the school week;
× is feasible in scope and within the resources of the school and community; and
× has an answer that will be important to the student and others.

Invite students to assess the overall quality of the inquiry questions they generated using the nine traits listed here. Ask for any questions related to their work on creating inquiry questions.

Then, invite students to try their hands at one or two webs of their own. They can work individually, in pairs, or in trios. Their task is to find potential pathways or real-world areas related to their interest topics and then generate an inquiry question. Share with them that you will be conferencing with each of them in the next phase of IBL, and that their thinking on webbing and inquiry questions ahead of time might prove beneficial. Assure students that you will continue to work with them wherever they are in the interest-focusing process.

FIGURE 5

Examples of Inquiry Questions In Need of Revision

Question	Reason for Revision	Revised Question
What are the least expensive menu options in local fast food restaurants?	Too narrow in focus; many answers are already known.	What are the reasons people go to/patronize fast food restaurants?
If children attend pre-school, are they better off when they get to kindergarten?	Too broad.	If children attend preschool for at least 1 year before entering kindergarten, do they enter kindergarten with stronger language skills than children who don't attend preschool?
What is imagination?	Too broad; may never have an answer.	What are current theories about creativity?
How many international air flights come into our airport each week?	Not open-ended.	What's the best layout of an airport that has international flights each day?
How can I save the polar bears?	Not feasible.	What efforts are being made by organizations around the world to save the polar bears?
How can I improve my skateboarding?	Not manageable.	What are the most effective practice routines for skateboarders who are beginners in the sport . . . have moderate experience . . . are experts?

"I really liked it when Mrs. Whitenberg came to our class to teach us about Coding Hour. Could I do a project where I just keep going with the lessons?"

—CARLA, GRADE 2

Conducting Your Next Round of Student Conferences

"Conferencing again?" you ask. Yes, indeed. In the first round of reflective conferences your goal was to ask clarifying questions of students, and your clarifying questions helped them to pinpoint their top two interests. In this round, you will be following similar steps to those you followed in the last round, and we are using LEGO bricks as an example of a student interest area.

Step 1: Preparing Students for Conferences

To make the most effective use of your time and to help ensure that you provide students with opportunities for ownership, ask each student to complete Resource 11: Developing My Inquiry Question Preconference Form.

Step 2: Scheduling Student Conferences

Schedule your students for 5- to 8-minute conferences during your IBL learning time as well as any regular class time that you can garner. Make sure students know when it is their turn with you and where you will meet with them.

Step 3: Preparing for Conferences

You do not need to do anything specific to prepare for this second round of conferences. With that said, it would certainly be advisable to have the traits of

Name: _____ Date: _____

Developing My Inquiry
Question Preconference Form

Directions: This preconference template is designed to help you prepare for your meeting with your teacher to find an inquiry question for your upcoming IBL project. Please complete as many of the questions as you can. If you cannot answer some, do not worry. You will complete them together during your conference time.

1. My top two interest areas based upon My Interests are:

   a. _____

   b. _____

2. Based upon my two top interests, I think I would like to research these areas:

   a. _____

   b. _____

   c. _____

3. Here are some questions that I might like to answer:

   a. _____

   _____

   b. _____

   _____

   c. _____

   _____

   d. _____

   _____

Name: _____ Date: _____

4. I need help with:

    a. _____
       _____

    b. _____
       _____

    c. _____
       _____

    d. _____
       _____

5. I want my teacher to help me with:

    a. _____
       _____

    b. _____
       _____

    c. _____
       _____

    d. _____
       _____

good inquiry questions handy, as well as your notebook or computer to complete note-taking at the conclusion of each conference.

Step 4: Conducting Conferences

Utilize the following steps:

1. **Ask a question.** We usually say something like, "Looks like you are interested in LEGO (or other topic). What do you especially like about LEGO?"

2. **Listen intently.** The student might say, "I like to build things," or "I like to make designs." Or "I like building complicated things because it feels great when I'm done." The student could also say, "I like to see if I can build taller and taller towers." Listen carefully because you might have made assumptions about the student's interest area. It might turn out that they have a whole other set of reasons for enjoying LEGO.

3. **Pose more focusing questions.** Based upon your careful listening, pose more clarifying questions. To the student who expressed a desire to build things, you might ask, "What else have you built?" For the student who liked to make designs, you might ask, "What is it about the designs that you especially like?" Similarly, for the student who liked the feeling of accomplishment when completing complicated tasks, you might ask, "What other complicated tasks have you completed?" or "Can you describe why it feels so good to you when you are done?" Finally, for the student who liked to build tall towers, you might ask, "Is it the tall towers that you like, or do you like being able to beat your own record?" Through all of this back-and-forth, you are attempting to uncover exactly why the student likes LEGO, or any other topic. By asking probing questions and listening, you are helping them pinpoint exactly what makes them passionate about an interest area.

4. **Paraphrase.** Reflect back to the student what you hear them say. Any time you need to get a "reality check" in this dialogue, paraphrase what you think the student is saying. Not only does paraphrasing assure your student that you are truly listening, but also it provides a check on your understanding of the student's real interests or important issues, which may or not be directly related to the topic suggested. A student's true interest area may be tangential to the topic identified on their interest survey. Finally, the occasional use of paraphrasing also allows you to keep the dialogue moving smoothly toward the desired end: an inquiry question based on the interest topic generated.

5. **Collaborate on an inquiry question.** Ask the student if they remember your large-group conversation about turning interest topics into inquiry questions. Hopefully, they remember. If not, no worries! Refresh their

thinking. You might say, "So, what do you think your inquiry question about LEGO would look like?" Once again, listen intently. Does the question the student posed meet their driving interest? Does it meet the attributes of an inquiry question laid out earlier? Is so, you have hit a home run. If the question needs tweaking, diagnose whether it misses the student's real interest and/or whether it does not reflect one or more of the traits of a solid inquiry question. Depending upon what a student says, you might need to ask additional questions.

6. **End with a smile.** Share an honest, positive comment about something specific that the student said, asked, and/or completed.

Step 5: Record-Keeping

Just as with the first round of conferences, keep track of your students' inquiry questions in your binder or wherever you are tracking students' progress.

CASE STUDIES
Andrea and Pablo

It is time to check in on the conference sessions with Andrea and Pablo, the two students you are following through this process. As expected, Andrea is pursuing an idea related to iMovie. Her conference was relatively easy because—without any prompting on your part—she shared that she wanted to research and learn the new features of the software and create an iMovie. You noted that in your record-keeping and told her to be thinking about a movie that incorporate the new features.

Pablo was not quite so easy. In your conference with him you had to draw out his recent reading about local environmental issues. Something had clicked with him when you asked him what local issues related to natural resources—air, water, land—he had come across in recent weeks. "My mother has been talking about the Flint, MI, water crisis and wondering if anything similar might be going on here with the treatment plant on our river," he shared. "Do you think there is anything to her suspicions?"

CASE STUDIES, CONTINUED

You replied that you did not know, but that it might prove a worthwhile investigation if he wanted to pursue it. You posed several ideas to him, including conducting some research about the temperatures in the river above and below the treatment plant. He looked interested because his eyes seemed to light up. You (1) told him to think seriously about the idea, (2) made a note of the idea in your record-keeping log, and (3) promised to meet with him again to confirm an inquiry question, such as "Is there a difference between the water temperature and chemical makeup of the river water above and below the local treatment plant?" You also (4) suggested that his next steps are to finalize his inquiry question and begin an action plan based on his selected inquiry question.

Conclusion

You have completed your second round of conferences for Step 2 of the IBL process, interest focusing. At this point, we believe you: (1) understand the nature of inquiry and inquiry questions, (2) can web real-world problem areas related to a student's interest area, (3) conduct reflective conferences to support student-generated inquiry questions, and (4) help students assess the overall quality of their inquiry question.

Looking forward, you will learn how to create an action plan for an IBL project in the next chapter. Action planning is Step 3 in the IBL process.

CHAPTER 7

Developing an Action Plan

The reason most people never reach their goals is that they don't define them, or ever seriously consider them as believable or achievable. Winners can tell you where they are going, what they plan to do along the way, and who will be sharing the adventure with them.

—Denis Waitley

The secret to getting ahead is breaking your complex, overwhelming tasks into small manageable tasks, and then starting on the first one.

—Mark Twain

You have finished your second round of conferences with each of your students, and that is a huge step forward. We assume, too, that at this point, each student and/or small groups of students has not only targeted an interest, but also explored and focused an inquiry question derived from that interest. This chapter explores the next step in the process: creating an action plan—collaboratively with students—for each project that is about to get underway.

After reading this chapter, you will be able to:

1. understand the importance of planning/initiating as a 21st-century skill;

2. articulate the connection between the action plan for an IBL project and initiation;

3. understand the significance of students' role in creating an action plan for their intended project;

4. use a template, My Action Plan (MAP), to collaboratively design an action plan for each student's IBL project;

5. conduct guided practice with students related to completing My Action Plan;

6. be able to differentiate in three different ways for students who may not be self-starters;

7. identify and use three techniques that can be used to help ensure student accountability for their learning; and

8. use Project Tracker, a teacher-friendly management form, to help ensure the success of students' investigations.

You may want to read the case study about Tyreke either before reading or after reading this chapter (see Appendix A). This case study features a real "go-getter" who needs support up front planning his initiative to ensure a successful completion.

Common Core State Standards and 21st-Century Learning Skills

Most educators continue to be guided by the CCSS or similar state standards, as well as other sets of standards put forward by content area councils, such as the NGSS and the C3 Framework. We discussed in Chapter 1 how IBL projects are aligned to these standards.

With that alignment as a backdrop, what do the CCSS say about the knowledge and skills students need to master? The CCSS "provide a clear understanding of what students are expected to learn . . . reflecting the knowledge and skills that our young people need for success in college and careers" (NGA & CCSSO, 2010a, 2010b). Although the knowledge—the content—defined within the CCSS is apparent, the skills that are imparted by the standards may be less apparent. Beyond the mastery of declarative knowledge, you need to be able to articulate the transferable skills with which students will leave high school.

We believe, as you probably do, that the CCSS include skills across both language arts and mathematics, such as communication, teamwork, problem solving, critical thinking, and research skills. Some skills, however, are simply outside the scope of the CCSS or other content area frameworks. To access these essential life skills that are required for successful careers in the Information Age, we turn to the 21st-century skills.

A dozen 21st-century skills were identified by a national coalition called the Partnership for 21st Century Learning (P21, 2019), and they are organized into three categories: learning, literacy, and life skills. The life skills include flexibility, leadership, initiative, productivity, and social skills. For IBL projects, we recommend focusing on initiative—a mindset and set of skills that come naturally to very few. Most students need lots of practice to become proficient initiators and planners.

We believe that today's students need to be introduced to the skills and mindset exhibited by adept initiators. Further, they need to be provided with multiple opportunities to initiate, manage, and own their learning, as well as be provided with timely and specific feedback if they are to graduate as competent and successful citizens in the Information Age. More than ever—and as practitioners with more than 100 years of combined experience—we believe that the most consequential learning occurs when students have recurring real-world opportunities to master knowledge and skills, see themselves as vitally connected to something that is personally meaningful, and see themselves as initiating and creating something that is new and unique to them. We believe that IBL—used systematically and iteratively—is a springboard to developing not only self-initiating young people, but also more engaged learners who have a strong sense of personal agency and are ready to launch successfully into the 21st century. Fullan et al. (2019) described these goals as the "new moral imperative of schools—one that puts learning, purpose and well-being—all on the same high pedestal" (p. 66).

What Is Initiative? What Is Planning?

Believe it or not, these two words—*initiative* and *planning*—are quite different, even though people might use them interchangeably in everyday conversations. Initiative, referring to a personal trait, has multiple meanings. Macmillan Dictionary defines it as the ability to decide in an independent way what to do and when to do it. The Oxford Dictionary states that initiative is the ability to assess and initiate things independently, the power or opportunity to act or take charge before others do. Still others define it as is the nature to take the first step in something. Finally, others suggest it is an important act or statement that is intended to solve a problem. Confusing? We believe for our work here with IBL that initiative is a combination of all of the definitions. It is an ability, refined over time, to solve complex problems or issues from beginning to end without managerial assistance.

Both Denis Waitley and Mark Twain, whose quotations opened this chapter, underscore that complexity. Once analyzed and defined, a seemingly insurmountable initiative—once broken down into smaller tasks—is within reach; the smaller tasks lend themselves to planning and action. To summarize, if you want your students to become initiators and self-starters, then you must support them in learning how to plan large projects effectively.

Action is also dependent upon a growth mindset, a belief that one gets smarter through hard work and the use of effective strategies and help from others when needed. You must concurrently work on developing these characteristics in students as well.

No wonder initiative is one of the hardest skills to learn and practice. It is complicated and multifaceted. And, no wonder initiative is one of the many highly sought abilities in students who will enter the 21st-century workplace!

Developing Planning/Initiative Skills Through an IBL Initiative

The tough question we must pose here is as follows: How often in today's classrooms are students provided with purposefully planned opportunities to utilize and refine their initiative? One could suggest that students are provided with hundreds of opportunities to self-start and complete assignments in every class they attend. Many would disagree with this notion, however, and suggest that—in actuality—students have not had many opportunities to practice this type of intentional planning because teachers often do this work ahead of time, defining deadlines, deliverables, and rubrics. Further, how often do students get targeted and timely feedback from their teachers regarding their planning skills, including their ability to self-start and complete successfully complex problems or projects? Teachers may simply assume that most students have picked up this skill and mindset just by being in school. But educators' assumptions may be working to students' disadvantage.

We believe that a well-structured IBL initiative will help to ameliorate this situation. Quite simply, an interest-based project, by its very nature, requires students to utilize their planning and initiative skills, develop a sense of agency, and share ownership for the learning journey. "But," you ask, "if they haven't had much practice with planning and initiative, let alone developing a sense of agency, how on earth do we even get them started?" Great question!

The first thing you have to do is to support students as they visualize initiative and planning. The next step is to provide them a with a template to assist them on their IBL journey. Our support and the visual planner in this chapter will help young people develop their initiative and planning skills.

In your next weekly session devoted to IBL, plan to set aside some time at the beginning of the time period to have a conversation with students about initiative. You can begin by sharing a story with them about a time when you needed to demonstrate initiative on a project. Describe the project for them, as well as how you needed a positive mindset to set out on the venture, set your goals, plan the steps and timeline to realize your goal, carry the steps out, and communicate your findings. Discuss the results of your work, as well as the reactions from your audience(s). Once you have finished your story, ask students, in a think-pair-share, to chat about the most important things that they heard you say. Next, debrief with them about the critical aspects of human initiative and/or planning. Finally, in a whole-class discussion, ask students, "What is easiest to do in an initiative of their own . . . hardest to do? Why might some aspects be easier than others? Why might some be harder than others?" Your goal in these discussions is to establish that initiating is a difficult and complex skill that requires practice.

Share with students that their IBL project will give them practice in developing initiative, as well as the feeling of satisfaction and agency as they move through all of the phases of their project. Assure them that they will not be "going it alone;" you will be there to meet with them, facilitate their work, provide feedback, and help to ensure that they complete the steps that they will each be setting for themselves, which they will begin crafting shortly. To help students visualize and move smoothly through all of the phases, use Resource 12: My Action Plan (MAP). An editable version of this template is available on the book's webpage.

At this point, provide students with an opportunity to review the template. Ask each student to work with a partner to analyze My Action Plan. Their question might be something like: "What does this remind me of that I have used in the past?" Debrief with your students. Your goal is threefold: to activate prior knowledge about their use of planning and initiating, gather information about the level of expertise of your students with planning and initiating as skills, and set the stage for guided practice.

Guided Practice With My Action Plan

Guided practice is one of Hunter's (1982) seven elements of effective instruction (i.e., objectives, standards, anticipatory set, teaching, guided practice, closure, independent practice), and it is interactive instruction between teacher and students. After you introduce new learning, you can begin the student practice process by engaging students in a similar task to what they will independently complete later in the lesson. If you want students to become proficient with a new skill or set

Name: _____ Date: _____

RESOURCE 12

My Action Plan (MAP)

My Action Plan (MAP)	**①** Goal	**②** Resources	**③** Steps and Timeline	**④** Product	**⑤** Criteria

My Interest Area: _____

Real-World Inquiry Question: _____

① **My goal:**

② **My resources:**
What I already know:

What I need to know to reach my goal:

The reading I need to do:

The Interest-Based Learning Coach © Prufrock Press Inc.

RESOURCE 12, CONTINUED

3 My first five steps (tasks/activities) to reach my goal and timeline:

1. _____
   Date Accomplished: _____

2. _____
   Date Accomplished: _____

3. _____
   Date Accomplished: _____

4. _____
   Date Accomplished: _____

5. _____
   Date Accomplished: _____

4 How I plan to communicate my findings (possible product formats):

5 How I know I've reached my goal (criteria for success if there are any at this point):

of skills, you need to provide an active application of the information with timely and targeted feedback to help ensure that they internalize the process.

Begin your guided practice by telling students that each of them will be responsible for completing their own MAP template. It is designed to help them initiate, monitor, and successfully complete their IBL project. Thus, they should listen closely as you are going to model how to complete the form with one or two volunteers from class.

With MAP in front of students or displayed for all students to see, ask for one or two volunteers from the class who are willing to share their interest area and ideas for targeted inquiry questions. When the volunteers are ready, work through the five areas on the template in sequence. Ask each volunteer to respond to the questions, and show students how the verbal answer provided would be notated on the document. For example, Andrea, introduced earlier, had a passion for movie making. She wanted to learn how to use the latest updates to iMovie. Her inquiry question was: "How can I successfully use and incorporate the special effects provided in iMovie?" Her goal for her MAP became: "Research the latest special effects in iMovie and create a film to showcase those features." Pablo, concerned about the water quality in the river that flowed through his neighborhood, decided he wanted to check the chemical composition and temperature of the river water north and south of the water treatment plant in town. His inquiry question was: "Does our water treatment plant's discharge impact the water quality in our river?" His goal became: "Research the water quality and temperature of the Androscoggin River water north and south of the treatment plant."

Continue through the questions until students have had a chance to see how responses are created and documented on all five questions on the template. Be sure to share that the steps listed in MAP apply to any endeavor they may initiate. Learning them now will help them in the future in any project they may undertake.

When your guided practice session is complete, provide students with 15–20 minutes to complete their first draft of MAP. Suggest to them that if they have trouble working forward with their action steps, it might be helpful to work backward from their desired outcome. Share with them, too, that in the next week or so you will be sitting with each student or small group of students to finalize each MAP. In this way, students become collaborators in the work that is getting underway. They will realize that they need to share responsibility for their learning and learning progress.

While students are working on their first draft of MAP, periodically check in with individual students. Provide feedback as necessary. Make sure to schedule all students for a subsequent conversation to review each action plan for comprehensiveness and reasonableness.

Levels of Support for Students in a Diverse Classroom

"You are joking," you exclaim. "What planet do you live on? Are you suggesting that everyone in my classroom will magically develop a full-blown sense of initiative and planning just by filling in answers to the questions on My Action Plan?"

> "I must admit that I like making my own topics in theory. I find it very exciting and love the idea of developing a topic and all the pieces fitting together, and it is beautiful! But at the end of the day, that never seems to happen for me. It's hard making good questions and following through on completing the project, even though I developed the topic myself. I need my teacher to help me along the way."
>
> **—JAVIER, GRADE 6**

Our answer is a resounding "no." We know absolutely that in today's diverse classrooms, there will always be a few self-starters who will be off and running. It will be difficult to keep them from charging ahead full steam, like Tyreke (see Appendix A). There will also be a group in the middle who may be slightly reluctant but willing to give IBL and MAP a try. At the same time, there will always be some students who simply do not have the confidence or the will to move ahead, like Cullen or Jared (see Appendix A). "What do I do now?" you ask.

Quite simply, you differentiate for those who do not have the readiness to initiate and plan as well as they might. There are three variables you can customize for diverse levels of readiness: (1) the number and size of the steps or actions on each student's MAP, (2) the frequency with which you check in with each individual or small group of students, and (3) the amount of feedback.

Let's go back to Andrea. If you are aware that she is a strong self-starter, you might be confident if she listed the following as her first five steps/actions on MAP:

1. Make a list of the special effects that I already know how to do.
2. Make a list of the special effects in iMovie that I do not yet know and would like to learn.
3. Develop a plan to learn each one.

4. Write a script for my new movie that incorporates each of the new special effects that I want to learn.
5. Film.

On the other hand, if you are aware that Andrea needs more direction to reach her goal, you would collaboratively plan together more detailed steps or sequenced actions. By making a more meticulous plan, you can be assured that each of the steps will lead successfully to the next, thereby avoiding confusion and disorder. Most importantly, you can be more confident that Andrea will experience success.

1. Make a list of the special effects that I already know how to do.
2. Visit the iMovie website to locate information about each of the new special effects included with the latest version of iMovie.
3. Write a brief summary of the new special effects that I want to learn.
4. Develop a plan, with a timeline, for learning about how to use each one (e.g., try a shoot using each special effect under different filming circumstances).
5. Brainstorm story plots that can incorporate one/more than one special effects.
6. Write a first draft of a script that incorporates the new special effects.
7. Create a story board for the different shoots that I plan.
8. Film.

To summarize, you can vary the number and magnitude of the steps contained within an action plan. Second, you can also vary the frequency with which you check in with students. For those who need more support than others, you can check in more frequently to ensure that progress is, indeed, on track. Finally, you can increase or decrease the amount of timely and specific feedback we provide to students. For those who might need a tad more support, you can increase your feedback. For those who are already self-starters and who seem to be on the right track, you can provide less.

These strategies will most likely work for 90% of students. But what about students who are so overwhelmed that they cannot get underway and distract the others in the class? Often, you need to collaborate with other building colleagues, such as specialists. Jared (see Appendix A) is one such student.

Supporting Student Responsibility and Accountability for Learning

"Okay," you say, "I think those ideas will help me address the differences in my students. But how can I help to ensure that students will demonstrate responsibility for their learning?" This may be one of the first times that students have ever had to plan and monitor their learning, let alone be held accountable for that learning.

Our combined field experiences suggest that there are at least three techniques you can try. The first is to provide a series of prompts to which students respond in a journal (see Figure 6 for some examples). The prompts can be daily, weekly, or whatever interval might address your needs. The benefits of this technique include students' practice with reflection and self-monitoring, as well as resulting data that you can use to pinpoint each student's progress. The drawback, of course, is that you will need to read, review, and respond in some way to these written responses.

The second technique is a verbal sharing during one of the weekly IBL time blocks. Once a month, for example, each student or small group of students should report to the whole class on one or two components of their work, for example: (1) what event/action/thinking helped them the most in their ongoing project and/or (2) what event/action/result was most challenging and how they solved it. The benefits of this technique include: (1) peer accountability for ongoing progress; (2) the fact that all students hear about successes, as well as challenges, and how the challenges were solved; and (3) that the oral presentations do not require additional teacher time to read. The drawback, if there is one, is that the oral presentations may cut into a portion of the weekly time allotted to the designated project work sessions.

The final technique for helping to ensure student accountability is a gallery walk. During the gallery walk every student must participate because each one reviews and makes notes about the successes and challenges showcased on the wall. Interestingly, our field experiences suggest that when students are reporting to their peers, they admit to feeling more pressured to make progress than when they only have to report to their teacher.

Keeping Track of Student Progress

"Oh, man," you holler, "This initiative is going to be like herding cats. I just know it. And I will have to be an octopus to keep everything moving forward!" Actually, no octopus is required here. We have designed an editable project tracking form

FIGURE 6

Journal Reflection Prompts

During the Initiating Stage:
- × When we first started talking about an IBL project, what was your initial thinking?
- × When we first started talking about the project, what was your initial feeling about working on a project like this?
- × Describe how you came up with your idea for a project.
- × Describe who or what helped you to decide on your topic.

During the Research Stage:
- × Once you focused on your topic, how did you decide on a product to share your work?
- × Once you focused on your topic, how did you conduct your research?
- × Describe your goals and the milestones that you set for your work. How did you stick to your timeframe? Did you deviate in any way? If so, explain.
- × How do you feel your project relates to real-world problems? How might your project help other people?
- × What were/are some of your challenges? How did you overcome them?
- × When did you experience success? What contributed to your success?
- × Explain how you helped others during your project work time.

As You Completed Your IBL Project:
- × What are some of the most interesting discoveries about your topic that you made along the way?
- × Explain two or three moments that made you most proud.
- × What things did you learn about yourself as you worked on your project?
- × Describe the three most important learning moments. These can be reflections about your topic, yourself and the way you work, and/or your peers.
- × What were some of the most challenging moments or problems that you encountered? Why were they challenging?
- × What strategies did you use to solve the most challenging problems?
- × What would you do differently if you approached this problem again?
- × What did you learn were your greatest strengths while you worked on your project?
- × Name one thing you learned about yourself and the way you work and/or learn that you want to improve?

FIGURE 6, CONTINUED

× How does working on an IBL project differ from other learning that you do in school?

× What advice would you give other students about working on a project like this?

× What more could my teacher have done to help me in all phases of my project?

× Provide two or three adjectives or adverbs that describe your work during project time.

× If you had the opportunity to do another project, would you undertake another? If so, why? If not, why not?

× At what point in your work did you feel like a genius? What made you feel that way?

that you can use to manage and keep track of student progress, and it is included in Resource 13: Project Tracker (also available on the book's webpage). Every time you sit with a student, record their progress and any important notes. Any time you need to check on or verify a student's status or progress, you simply access your records, whether they are in handwritten form or electronic.

Note that the Project Tacker has a different purpose than the formative assessment menus we provided in Chapter 4. The purpose of the Project Tracker form is twofold. First, it is designed so that you can notate periodically where students are regarding their projected learning journey in an IBL initiative (e.g., on track, not quite on target, ahead of plan). Second, it gives you the opportunity to note those students who need more support with respect to their timelines.

Conclusion

This chapter discussed how to develop a plan for each student's IBL project. Using MAP, each student should now have a plan that includes goals and an initial timeline for beginning their investigation. You have come a long way

In the next chapter, you will forge ahead. In Step 4 of the IBL process, students will become fledgling researchers as they begin to locate and gather their resources.

RESOURCE 13
Project Tracker

1. Student's interests:

   a. _____

   b. _____

   c. _____

2. Student's goals:

   a. _____

   b. _____

   c. _____

3. Student's inquiry question derived from their goals:

   _____

4. Student and teachers will integrate the following literacy standards, 21st-century skills, and social and emotional learning goals:

   a. _____

   _____

   b. _____

   _____

   c. _____

   _____

Name: _____ Date: _____

5. Initial action steps with target completion dates:

Action Steps	Target Date for Completion	Status (e.g., Not Started, Started, Done)

6. Conference notes:

Date	Notes

CHAPTER 8

Finding and Managing Resources

What gets us in trouble is not what we don't know. It's what we know that just ain't so.

—Mark Twain

At this point, you are well underway with your IBL initiative. If you began at the start of the school year, you are probably into late October or early November, 6–8 weeks into the IBL process. Students will have identified their interests, analyzed and narrowed down an inquiry question, and developed an action plan (MAP) to guide their upcoming work. In this chapter, you will support students as they begin their actual research, searching for and using a variety of resources. If you are following the IBL process, you are now ready to explore resources (Step 4).

As students begin their investigations, they will already have thought about what reading they have yet to do. This was a question on their action plan. Beyond initial reading, however, there are many other resources that students will use in their ongoing investigations. Resources are sources of knowledge for students and teachers. They should provoke thinking and promote clarity of understanding about the investigation at hand.

After reading this chapter, you will be able to:

1. understand the difference between primary and secondary sources and the significance of the difference for students' IBL projects;
2. identify different types of resources within the school and wider community;

3. keep an ongoing and systematic record of school and community resources; and

4. manage and support how students use a wide variety of 21st-century resources and determine each one's credibility.

Primary and Secondary Resources

Resources are categorized into two types: primary and secondary. A primary source provides firsthand evidence about an event, object, or person. It includes the original materials on which other research is based and, as such, aids students to get as close as possible to what actually happened at the time in question. Primary sources reflect an individual's viewpoint and can be written or nonwritten (e-mails, letters, sound, pictures, artifacts, etc.). Examples include, but are not limited to:

- × artifacts of all kinds, such as tools, coins, clothing, furniture, etc.;
- × audio recordings, DVDs, and video recordings;
- × autobiographies and memoirs;
- × diaries, personal letters, and correspondence;
- × eyewitness accounts;
- × government documents (reports, bills, proclamations, hearings, etc.);
- × Internet communications on e-mail, blogs, LISTSERVs, and newsgroups;
- × interviews, surveys, and fieldwork;
- × official and unofficial records of organizations and government agencies;
- × original documents (birth certificates, property deeds, trial transcripts);
- × patents;
- × poetry;
- × political cartoons;
- × photographs, drawings, and posters;
- × public opinion polls;
- × research data, such as census statistics;
- × scientific journal articles reporting experimental research results;
- × speeches and oral histories;
- × technical reports;
- × coins;
- × tools;
- × laws; and
- × plant or animal specimens.

Unlike primary sources, secondary sources characterize, talk about, clarify, comment upon, analyze, examine, condense, and/or process primary sources. Thus, a secondary source is generally one or more steps removed from the event or time period and is written or produced after the fact with the benefit of hindsight. In all likelihood, the author was not a participant in the event in question. Like primary sources, secondary materials can be written or nonwritten (sound, pictures, movies, etc.), and examples of secondary sources include, but are not limited to:

- × bibliographies;
- × biographical works;
- × documentaries;
- × commentaries and treatises;
- × history books and other popular or scholarly books;
- × literature reviews and review articles (e.g., movie reviews, book reviews);
- × reference books, including dictionaries, encyclopedias, and atlases;
- × television broadcasts;
- × textbooks; and
- × works of criticism and interpretation.

The distinction between these two kinds of resources is important to understand as students pursue their research questions. Students' use of primary or secondary sources hinges on the type of research they are conducting. For example, if a student is interested in public perceptions related to the most recent presidential campaign, political cartoons, or op-ed columns would be good primary source documents. A secondary source on the most recent presidential campaign would be a newspaper article or book on campaign finance reform. If a student is interested in music, for example, a primary source might include the score of a musical or an original composition. A secondary source would include a biography about a composer or lyricist. Clearly, students need to be aware of the proximity of the resource to the event and, equally important, any bias of an author who may be interpreting an event, work of art, etc.

With this information about primary and secondary sources in hand, it is essential to begin your own record of school and community resources. Kept track of in an ongoing fashion, the recorded resources will prove invaluable information to teachers and students as they pursue IBL initiatives over the years. For our purposes, we divided Resource 14: Resource Record Template into five categories: (1) people, (2) other living things, (3) natural resources, (4) within-school resources, and (5) community resources. Should you believe there are other important categories to include, you can add them into the rows in the editable template for this resource that is included on the book's webpage.

RESOURCE 14

Resource Record Template

Directions: Use this table to keep a running record of the resources students can utilize in their IBL projects. The resources can be categorized into five areas:

1. **People** include building teachers, teachers within the district, custodial staff, secretaries, central office administrators, former students, graduates, community senior citizens, community experts, national experts, etc.

2. **Living things** include animals, plants, trees, flowers, amphibians, pets, fish, etc.

3. **Natural resources** include lakes, streams, oceans, minerals, air, wood.

4. **Within-school resources** include laboratories, computer labs, the library, a greenhouse or garden, kitchens, woodworking or engineering equipment, and copy machines.

5. **Community resources** might include any or all of the following: businesses and industries, roadways, town offices, the local library, the post office, local community colleges, universities, hospitals, and private schools.

Blank spaces have been provided under each to facilitate your own listings. Use this as a template and modify it to fit your needs, now and in the future.

Resource	Contact Name	Address	Phone	Notes
People				
Living Things				
Natural Resources				
Within School				
Community Resources				

The Teacher's Role: Resource Acquisition in the 21st Century

As a facilitator of student projects, you have a critically important role to play related to resource acquisition. Your role goes way beyond the traditional one in which teachers simply helped students locate and check out print material in the library. In a 21st-century IBL initiative, you will be the facilitator and manager for a wide array of resources. Thus, you may find yourself initiating and completing a range of managerial duties, depending upon the resource type being sought. The following are just a few examples of the types of tasks in which you might engage:

1. locating primary source documents;
2. researching, locating and securing video clips;
3. making initial contact with a community member on behalf of a student who requires information from an expert in a particular area;
4. calling a local TV/radio station to locate a broadcast/transcript/recording of a past broadcast;
5. calling a local/state/national newspaper to find out how to secure permission for a student to use a news story/political cartoon, etc.;
6. providing mini-lessons on how to cite a source and create properly formatted list of references; and/or
7. seeking out and contacting a communications director of a local business to find out how a student might be able to request an interview with an employee.

Note that when students are researching an inquiry question, they often need to consider student safety (e.g., professional qualifications of expert/mentor; cost, if any; criteria for involvement; length of response time).

"You want me to contact a real man—this senator—who actually listened to Martin Luther King speak? You mean, REALLY? You mean ME? Why would this real, important man care about me? I'm just a student. Would he really talk to someone like me?"

—TYREKE, GRADE 8

The Teacher's Role: Determining the Credibility of Resources

If you are earnest about preparing students for this century, then one of the most important tasks you have related to resource acquisition is helping students determine the credibility and reliability of information. Mark Twain, whose quotation opens this chapter, captured our current dilemma aptly. The Information Age is—at one and the same time—a blessing and a curse. Students have instant access to a "fire hydrant" of information on every topic. At the same time, and as a practitioner, you are obligated to help students use critical thinking to weed out the inaccurate, biased, and misleading information that comes with the wealth of information.

"I have to deal with this, too?" you ask. "Yes, emphatically, yes!" is our answer. Every teacher should share responsibility for helping students make reasoned judgments about the overall quality of information. Why? Research shows that students are more concerned about content relevance than credibility and, as a result, rarely attend to the author, publication type, or context (Coiro, 2014; Pilgrim et al., 2019). More alarming, Stanford researchers found that students displayed a "stunning and dismaying consistency" in their responses, the researchers wrote, "getting duped again and again" (Wineburg et al., 2016). The researchers were not looking for high-level analysis of data but just a "reasonable bar" of, for instance, distinguishing fake accounts from real ones, activist groups from neutral sources, and ads from articles.

Most important to every teacher is that "assessing the credibility and accuracy of multiple sources of information" is at the heart of the CCSS writing standards. Based on this backdrop, you have a win-win opportunity to embed several mini-lessons about the notions of multiple perspectives, new ways of thinking about 21st-century content, and specific strategies to promote healthy skepticism about any information. You can conduct these mini-lessons during the time you have set aside for interest-based learning, regular classroom time, or both.

With the CCSS standards as a backdrop, it is time to destress. All teachers are responsible for teaching these skills, and, thus, you are not alone. Work with your colleagues to share responsibility for teaching these standards. Your collegial sharing will help to reduce your workload and strengthen professional relationships.

To get you started, we are including two helpful resources. The first, Table 5, contains several video clips that we have curated for your use with students about the credibility of resources. Although there are hundreds of reasonably short videos available online that you could use if you had the time to cull them yourself, we thought these were noteworthy. You may use any one of these to jumpstart conversations with the whole class or small groups of students. You might even use any or

TABLE 5
Video Clips: Determining Source Credibility

Video	URL	Length	Grade	Summary
Evaluating Sources for Credibility	https://www.youtube.com/watch?v=PLTOVoHbH5c	3:15	3+	This short video answers three questions: What does it mean for a source to be credible? Why is it important to use sources that are credible? How can you tell if a source is credible?
How to Evaluate Resources	https://www.youtube.com/watch?v=bZ122WakNDY	5:10	3+	The narrator, Nerd Squirrel, shares five strategies for evaluating resources: author, audience, review process, currency, and perspective.
Evaluating Sources on the World Wide Web	https://www.youtube.com/watch?v=ELclOOxzt3U	7:26	5+	This comprehensive clip walks through five steps to assess webpages: (1) examine the URL, (2) scan the page, (3) look for quality markers, (4) find out what others say, and (5) does it all add up?
Source Credibility: The T.R.A.P. Method	https://www.youtube.com/watch?v=w4RygY6tjWw	2:54	3+	The TRAP method invites students to look at the Timeliness, Reliability, Authorship, and Purpose of a source to assess its credibility.
Good vs Bad Sources	https://www.youtube.com/watch?v=5TPlvTpHJWw	1:26	3+	A very short PowToon clip that features three questions students should ask: Who wrote it? Who published it? What's the URL?
Exploring	https://www.eduscapes.com/sessions/middle/3.htm	N/A	5+	This is not a video clip. Rather, it is a comprehensive website that addresses the world of inquiry in the 21st century. Part III focuses on collecting resources and interviewing experts, among other topics.

all of them as station activities. Each row of the table contains the video title that is embedded with the link, the length of the clip, its grade-level appropriateness, and a brief summary.

Second, we have created a list of questions, outlined in Resource 15: Questions for Determining Credibility, that students can use as prompts when they read source material. You will note that the questions are divided into five categories, similar to those that are featured in the video clips in Table 5. Please customize it for your purposes and the needs of your students (see book's webpage).

Whenever students read the content of a primary or secondary source, they should be simultaneously thinking critically about the nature of the resource. We recognize that students will not always answer every question with each resource. We do believe, however, that with the right modelling, repetition, and conversation, you can support students to become more critical readers and begin to reverse that "dismaying" inability referenced earlier, to distinguish neutral sources from biased ones and fake accounts from real ones.

Conclusion

Students have access to unimaginable amounts of information today, which they need as they pursue an IBL project. The Internet provides a limitless research tool that can be students' best friend or worst enemy. Accessing information is easy; accessing credible and reliable information tends to be more complicated, as Mark Twain's quotation—at the opening of this chapter—attests. Students need to be taught how to sift through the millions of webpages available on a topic and find what they need (and be able to trust what they find).

In this chapter, we considered a wide variety of resources and showcased two different ways to categorize them. One is not necessarily better than other; they are simply two different, yet important, ways to use resources. We also talked about the teacher's role as a manager of resources in an IBL initiative. Without a doubt, managing resources is a critical role. Not only will you have to locate and systematize school and community resources across the years in IBL cycles, but also you will have to model and support the critical thinking that is required if students are to be successful with their project *and* savvy digital citizens in the 21st century. The next chapter focuses on the researching, investigating, exploring, experimenting, and designing that students will complete during the IBL process.

RESOURCE 15 ━━━━
Questions for Determining Credibility

Category	Questions
Author	× Who wrote this? Why should I trust them? × In what way is the author/authors associated with this topic? × Does this represent the author's opinion or fact? × What expertise or experience does the author have? × What perspectives does the author represent? × What does the author use to support their perspective? × What biases might the author have regarding this topic? How does this impact what is being said? × With what institutions is this author associated?
Currency	× When was it written, and why does that date matter? × Has anything changed in this field of study since the publication date?
Purpose	× What is the intent of the information?
Audience	× Who is the intended audience?
Publisher	× Where and how was this published? × Is what I'm looking at where this was originally published, or did it originate elsewhere? × What are the publisher's/organization's objectives? How might this impact content or bias? × Does this source contain citations? Who else is cited within the content, and are those sources themselves credible?

CHAPTER 9

Research, Development, and Design

Creativity requires input, and that's what research is. You're gathering material with which to build.

—Gene Luen Yang

The word *research* has a 400-year history. It is derived from two French words, *re*, meaning "intense force," and *cerchier*, meaning "to search." In today's world, we define research as the act of searching closely, or methodical investigation and study of objects, components, processes, and sources. Its current purpose is to identify facts or discover new findings.

Unfortunately, many traditional, school-based independent study and research projects do not adhere to that definition, and instead, ask students to rephrase, rehash, reword, and restate, with little or no opportunity for close examination, discovery, or investigation. The introduction of problem-based learning, project-based learning, Genius Hour, passion projects, and Makerspaces attempts to break this artificial and constrained pattern by reinforcing and introducing elements of creativity, design, and experimentation, coupled with personal choices. Research then becomes the purpose of the IBL process or a preparatory aspect that is used prior to design and model building.

This chapter fosters the use of an authentic definition of research. Its five interdependent sections begin with a description of real-world research and its purpose. Next, we link students' IBL research and design with related and compelling state standards in language arts, science, and social studies. Using these two foundational elements, we consider the different kinds of authentic research students might pursue when participating in IBL. The fourth section of this chapter focuses on the research process and its various elements. Most importantly, we discuss strategies for encouraging students to use their research as a base for new perspectives, alternative approaches and solutions, and creativity.

In an effort to make this book's explanations and suggestions clear and organized, we arranged each section of this chapter using the following goals. If you want to review all of the text's information about the IBL research and design process, you should read the chapter sequentially. You may also choose to search for chapter goals, questions, and segments that best align with your students' needs and interests.

After reading this chapter, you will be able to:

1. define research and design;
2. link IBL research and design with standards for language arts, science, and social studies;
3. review the different kinds of research and design protocols students might pursue during IBL;
4. describe the research and design process; and
5. explain various strategies that promote research and design as a precursor for new perspectives, solutions, products, services, and creativity.

What Is the "Real" Definition of Research, and Why Is It Relevant for IBL?

The Oxford Dictionary defines research as "the systematic investigation into and study of materials and sources in order to establish facts and reach new conclusions." Oxford also offers synonyms that include investigation, experimentation, testing, exploration, analysis, fact-finding, and examination.

Researchers and education specialists from the 1930s (Dewey, 1938) through the 1990s (Newmann & Wehlage, 1995) and the first decade of the 20th century (Rule, 2006) have also contributed their perspectives about the definition of authentic student research. Specifically, Newmann and Wehlage explained such real-world research as a composite of seven factors. First, students organize, synthesize, interpret, explain, or evaluate complex information in order to address a concept, problem, or issue. They also review, propose, or investigate various solutions, strategies, perspectives, or points of view related to their issue. This work allows them to demonstrate their understanding of the essential concepts and principles that bind an academic discipline. Fourth, student researchers use communication, collaboration, inquiry, and research methods typically found in that discipline. Students also demonstrate the ability to elaborate on their new understandings through oral, written, or media-based communication. Most importantly, authentic student research involves an authentic concept, need, issue, or problem that learners are likely to encounter in a community outside of their families and classrooms. Specific to the nature of the concept or problem, and the related knowledge and skills acquired during the research process, students then communicate their knowledge to a relevant and involved audience. Alternately, students who research authentic concepts and issues take action to address or explain their findings. These dimensions and their related guiding questions are categorized and listed in Table 6. You might be interested in using these key features and guiding questions to identify the aspects of a student's goal that may need refinement, extensions, coaching, or redirection.

Educators who are concerned about the ritualistic and rote conception of research used in many classrooms wholeheartedly support the more authentic definitions expressed by the Oxford Dictionary and these researchers. They endorse efforts to encourage original research and see it as a worthy goal. But is this kind of authentic research practical within a classroom or schoolwide setting? Is "real" research developmentally appropriate for a primary grade classroom? And, does this conception of research align well with the design goals inherent in IBL models, such as Makerspaces?

An examination of Oxford's synonyms for research (i.e., investigation, experimentation, testing, exploration, analysis, fact-finding, and examination) and Newmann and Wehlage's (1995) focus on real-world concepts, problems, or issues provides a means for addressing these questions. Consider the sample student IBL goals we originally shared in Chapter 4 (see Table 3, p. 47). At face value, all of the students' interests seem personally relevant, and their goals and questions appear to be developmentally appropriate for the individual child. Jesse's and Jade's IBL goals seem as if they are likely to result in an IBL project that could align with all of the aspects contained in the Oxford definition and in Newmann and Wehlage's (1995) focus areas. Their work provides for the development of new knowledge, problem solving, solution finding, and communication with a relevant real-world audience.

Jamal's Tappan Zee Bridge project aligns well with Oxford's "study of materials," "exploration," and "reach new conclusions" expectations. Given his previous work at home, in the community, and at school with design and model building, this new goal is also in his individual zone of proximal development (Vygotsky, 1978).

Consider the same alignment exercise with Esteban's kitchen chemistry goal. With the proper safety precautions and grade-appropriate materials, it is an appropriate goal for his age. It is doubtful that his work will produce any knowledge that

TABLE 6

Key Features of an Authentic Interest-Based Learning Goal

Dimension	Guiding Question
Personal Interest	Is this topic, question, or goal a new, developing, or long-term student interest?
Developmentally Appropriate	Can the student's interest and goal be addressed in a scaffolded manner that is in keeping with their prior knowledge and cognitive level?
Complex Information	Does this question or goal address a concept, materials, problem, or issue that is considered complex for the student's age or experience level?
Reasoning	Will the student's research work involve gathering information or data from multiple sources, as well as organizing, synthesizing, interpreting, explaining, and/or evaluating information?
Content Understanding	Does this research or inquiry project offer an opportunity for the student to demonstrate their understanding of the essential concepts, materials, and skills within the relevant discipline?
Real-World Methodology	Will this project allow students to simulate or apply the research, investigation, exploration, design, collaboration, inquiry, and communication methods within its related discipline?
Research-Based Products	Does the research incorporate, or culminate in, an information review, a proposal, an investigation, or the development of solutions, strategies, or a new perspective?
Research Communication	Will the student, or small group of students, have the opportunity to share their research findings with a relevant and involved audience through oral, written, or media-based communication?
Authenticity	Does the research goal or question align with an authentic concept, need, issue, or problem that learners are likely to encounter in a community outside of their families and classrooms?

is new to the world as a whole. It will, however, allow for the development of new science understandings and methods for Esteban, and for his audience of interested young scientists. It also addresses the experimentation and investigation expectations as well as a focus on methods and communication to a relevant audience.

In a similar fashion, Fredo's, Evan's, and CJ's music, coding, and wild edibles projects stem from their own interests and support the development of authentic methods in their chosen disciplines. Lastly, Rob's and Daeun's design goals, one in the field of art and another in construction, also allow for the development of authentic methods and skills. Both project ideas allow students to work in their interest area, on a goal of their choosing, and as novices who simulate the work of adult researchers and designers.

We submit that with proper attention to interest-focusing and provisions for careful project planning, scaffolding, and coaching, IBL projects can support goals related to authentic inquiry. When considered as complementary frameworks and models, Genius Hour, passion projects, Makerspaces, and the IBL framework embody the prevailing conceptions of authentic student research.

How Does IBL Research Align With the CCSS?

Let's move from an examination of the key features of authentic research to a review of the CCSS. Do they address research as well? And if so, in what manner? Lastly, how does state standards' vertical progress define developmental appropriateness?

The CCSS-ELA incorporate research standards, specifically within each grade level's writing strands (NGA & CCSSO, 2010a). Most states have either adopted the CCSS or created very similar versions of the standards for use in their particular state. For example, in kindergarten through grade 2, students are expected to participate in shared research and writing projects, as well as to gather information from experiences or provided sources in order to answer a question. Between kindergarten and grade 2, the standards anticipate decreasing levels of support and collaboration. By grade 3, students are expected to conduct short research projects using multiple print and digital resources independently.

This progression continues through grade 12, with grade 8 students continuing to conduct short research, analysis, or reflection projects to answer multiple, relevant, focused, and self-generated questions that generate other avenues for exploration (NGA & CCSSO, 2010a). Eighth-grade students are also expected to use search terms and determine credibility and accuracy as they identify relevant, multiple sources related to their research question. In the written communication of their findings, students must avoid plagiarism by quoting accurately as appropriate and paraphrasing.

The literacy standards for history are identical to the generic language arts standards. The science and technical area standards incorporate similar expectations but also call for students to integrate quantitative and technical information with both words and a visual representation. In addition, they are expected to make judgments based on research findings and to compare information from experiments, simulations, and multimedia sources (NGA & CCSSO, 2010a).

The NGSS (NGSS Lead States, 2013) and the C3 Framework (NCSS, 2013) also integrate the CCSS grade-level research standards within their expectations for content literacy, so those literacy-related research demands for each grade level remain the same. In addition to the inquiry expectations for both science and social studies, the science standards incorporate experimentation, design, model building, data collection, and analysis. Table 7 provides a chart that lists the ever expanding research skill expectations for students between kindergarten and grade 8.

This brief review of the language arts, science, and social studies standards makes it clear that research expectations are embedded throughout all three sets of standards. For this reason, the integration of national standards with students' IBL projects may be seamless—if the student researchers have already demonstrated mastery of their grade level's language arts, science, and social studies research standards.

If not, you will need to decide which grade-level research standards, if any, you want to incorporate in a student's IBL goals and plans. You may be willing to accept less than grade-level evidence for some students' IBL projects. In other cases, the state research standards may not apply to a given project. In yet other instances, small-group projects may provide the scaffolding that some students need to meet the demands of these standards. Lastly, you may be willing to add mini-lessons, modeling, video coaching, or tip sheets, in the form of checklists and examples, to help students learn the new aspect of their grade-level research standards.

What Kinds of Research Might Students Conduct During the IBL Process?

As we mentioned at the beginning of this chapter, research involves an intense search. But a search for what? Based on our experiences, there are at least three

TABLE 7
An Analysis of the Research-Related Assessment Tasks in the NGSS Performance Expectations

Kindergarten	Grade 3	Grade 5	Middle School
Analyze data.	Obtain and combine information.	Make observations and measurements.	Collect, synthesize, analyze, and interpret data.
Plan and conduct an investigation.	Make measurements.	Measure and graph data.	Construct and interpret graphical and visual data displays.
Use tools and materials.	Make, use, and share observations.	Analyze and interpret data.	Ask questions about data.
Evaluate a design model.	Represent data in tables and graphs.	Represent patterns in data.	Plan and conduct an investigation.
Construct an argument with evidence.	Define a design problem.	Conduct an investigation.	Evaluate an experimental design and a design solution.
Use a model.	Develop models.	Support an argument.	Conduct iterative testing and modifications.
Ask questions.	Use evidence to support an explanation.		Define criteria and constraints.
Communicate solutions.	Make a claim about a solution.		Design a method, solution, and a device.
			Describe, develop, and use a model.
			Undertake a design project to construct, test and modify a solution and a device.
			Construct and support an explanation with evidence.
			Use argument, evidence, and reasoning.
			Integrate information to support claims.

purposes and three different kinds of research that engage students during the IBL experience. We have organized these categories based on the student's IBL goals and inquiry questions.

Some student's IBL goals are to become more knowledgeable or more skillful. We have used the term *information research* to describe this category. Information research questions can be answered through the use of secondary sources (e.g., reference books, articles, webpages, and nonfiction text), as well as through access to knowledgeable others. As an example, consider Jesse (see p. 47) and his interest in the Great Pacific Garbage Patch. If Jesse's goal is to become more informed about this topic, then research with secondary sources can meet his need. On the other hand, if a preliminary review of secondary sources compels Jesse to speak with or meet local people with expertise in this area, then he will extend his research to include primary resources (e.g., experts, photographs, journals, surveys, artifacts, observations, videoclips, audio, interviews, etc.).

We suggest that Evan's interest in learning how to code and Fredo's interest in music lessons are also examples of information research. Both Evan and Fredo had assistance from knowledgeable others (the music and the technology teachers). They also used secondary sources for their research (e.g., music books and coding instruction sites). Like many learners, all three of these students were familiar with the information research process, as it is the primary type of research conducted in schools. However, none of these three students had much interest in sharing their learning with others or in developing a research-based product. Their learning goal was strictly confined to information finding.

Investigations, observations, and experimentation comprise the second category of student research. With our learners, we often referred to it as *experimental research*. Related student goals center on the development of new knowledge or data, or a new perspective. This kind of student research begins with the formation of a hypothesis or inquiry question, followed by experimentation or observation linked to the hypothesis. Data collection, data analysis, and the drawing of conclusions follow. Examples include Jade's IBL goal related to college and professional baseball player statistics, as well as CJ's pursuit to locate and experiment with wild edibles.

Both researchers conducted information research prior to developing their hypothesis or inquiry question. They also collected and organized the data they collected to answer their inquiry question. Jade used a statistical analysis to answer her research question, and CJ organized and described the new data she collected. Both student researchers were interested in developing a product related to their investigations; in one case, it was a data chart coupled with informative text. In the other case it was an illustrated booklet. Both were agreeable to sharing their work with interested others, although this was not part of their original IBL goal.

The third type of IBL research involves goals related to modeling, design, invention, construction, and fabrication. Creativity, expression, representation, and the development of new products and processes are at the heart of these students' learning goals. Daeun's IBL goal regarding watercolors, Jamal's Tappan Zee Bridge model, and Rob's cabinet construction are examples of this category. Additional examples might include students interested in building a functional model of a better backpack, or a new toy for infants. Popular culture often describes this type of research as *tinkering* or *making* (Martinez & Stager, 2013). Students involved in the development or representation of new products and processes are also likely to begin their work with information research. These efforts increase their knowledge base and make them aware of the important facts, concepts, and skills that are likely to be useful during their design and development phase.

You may find it helpful to illustrate and explain the three different types of research to the students who are participating in an IBL initiative. Table 8 supports this effort. It lists each of these three categories. It contains sample student goals, questions, resources, and examples. A brief mini-lesson might name the three types and provide examples of each. Students can be encouraged to add to the list of relevant goals, questions, and examples. We further suggest that the explanation not express any bias for one type of research over another. Merely describing and explaining the three types should be sufficient to help students understand and pinpoint their own research goals and next steps.

Why is it important to understand and communicate the various types of research that students might pursue? First, knowledge of other types of research and other examples often broadens students' horizons and opens their minds to new possibilities for their own future work. Second, it helps them understand that, although far-reaching and important, information research, with its numerous "Googleable" answers, is not the only type of interest-based work supported and endorsed in the IBL environment. Third, the identification of the research categories helps both teachers and students select the appropriate pathway and step for the ensuing research process.

What Are the Steps of the Research and Design Process?

The steps and process for information, investigative, and tinkering/design research are similar, but not identical. Table 9 names each research category and describes the process for each. All three types of research begin with the selection and naming of a learning goal and an inquiry question. Chapters 6 and 7 focused

TABLE 8
Three Research Design Categories With Student Examples

	Information Finding		
Question	What are . . . all about?	How do people . . . ?	Why did . . . happen?	What are the ways I could . . . ?
Goal	I want to know all about . . .	I want to learn how to . . .	I want to be an expert on . . .	I want to find out . . .
Resources	Reference books	Nonfiction books	Websites	Experts
Examples	Micah wants to learn about great white sharks.	Evan wants to learn how to code.	Marisa wants to read about famous women.	Fredo wants to learn how to play music.

	Experimental Research and Investigation		
Question	Is there a pattern for . . . ?	How can I analyze data about . . . ?	Is . . . better than . . . ?	What is the relationship between . . . and . . . ?
Goal	I want to compare data about . . .	I want to collect information about . . .	I want to do an experiment about . . .	I want to investigate . . .
Resources	Primary sources	Secondary sources	Raw data	Technology
Examples	Jade wants to do a math experiment with baseball statistics	CJ wants to collect and study wild plants.	Esteban wants to do science experiments.	Arjun wants to interview soldiers who served in Vietnam.

TABLE 8, CONTINUED

		Tinkering, Designing, and Making		
Question	How can I improve . . . ?	Can I make a _____ that illustrates . . . ?	Can I use tools and materials to make a . . . ?	Can a model help people understand more about . . . ?
Goal	I want to make a better . . .	I want to design a	I want to build a	I want to make a model that explains . . .
Resources	× Reference books × Nonfiction text and articles × Experts in the field × Tools × Raw materials	× Reference books × Nonfiction text and articles × Experts in the field × Tools × Raw materials	× Reference books × Nonfiction text and articles × Experts in the field × Tools × Raw materials	× Reference books × Nonfiction text and articles × Experts in the field × Tools × Raw materials
Examples	Sophia wants to design a better backpack.	Daeun wants to create a watercolor painting.	Rob wants to design plans and a blueprint to build a cabinet.	Jamal wants to make a model of the Tappan Zee Bridge.

TABLE 9
Three Research Processes

The Information Research Process

Phase 1	Phase 2	Phase 3	Phase 4	Phase 5	Phase 6
× Select a topic and question that interests you. × Make sure you can manage it in the time you have.	× Decide on the keywords and phrases that might guide your information research. × Do a quick search to see if you can find the information you want.	× Revise your question and goal based on your trial run research. × Locate the materials and sources you need to answer your question.	× Use your resources and materials to gather information about your topic and question. × Take notes. × Make a list of your sources.	× Review your notes. × Find and list the main ideas your research uncovered. × Organize your notes according to these main ideas. × Create a sequence for your main ideas that makes sense. × Use this sequence to organize your writing.	× Write a rough draft explaining your main ideas and details. × Use your own words. Do not copy your resources. × Place transitions between main ideas. × Add an introduction and conclusion. × Cite your sources. × Revise the rough draft. × Share your learning with interested others.

TABLE 9, CONTINUED

The Investigation and Experimentation Research Process					
Phase 1	**Phase 2**	**Phase 3**	**Phase 4**	**Phase 5**	**Phase 6**
× Select your research topic. × Name your rough idea for an inquiry question or a hypothesis.	× Research your problem or question. × Find out what others have learned. × Revise your goal, inquiry question, or hypothesis based on your information research.	× Plan your investigation methods. × Find the materials, places, people, and tools you need. × Do a "dry run" to work out the kinks in your plan.	× Conduct your investigation or experiment. × Collect the data.	× Organize your data. × Analyze your data. × Decide if you reached your goal. Decide how the data link to your hypothesis. × Summarize your data.	× Explain your study. × Describe how the study answers your research question. × Draw conclusions from the data. × Make recommendations for further research.

The Tinkering and Design Process					
Phase 1	**Phase 2**	**Phase 3**	**Phase 4**	**Phase 5**	**Phase 6**
× Name your goal or your problem. × Name your purpose and the ways you will judge your work.	× Collect information about your goal and topic. × Find out about the work others have done in this area.	× Use the information you find to identify, describe, and sketch possible pathways and solutions toward your goal.	× Develop a draft of your design or product. × Test your model or design. × Look for weak points and remedy them.	× Share the draft with others. × Get their feedback. × Use the feedback to improve your product.	× Prepare the best version of your design, model, or product. × Present your design to others and explain its purpose and benefits.

on this topic in depth. These conversations and coaching opportunities prepare students for the next phase of the research process. This generally involves either a preliminary or a thorough search for related primary and secondary information sources and the information they can provide related to the interest area, goal, and inquiry question.

The third phase of the research process involves revision of the original research question or research planning, the location of materials and tools, or the design or the creation of a rough draft. These preliminary steps pave the way for the reading and note gathering typical during an information research project. In a similar vein, students involved in an investigation or experiment use this fourth phase to conduct their experiment or to investigate the phenomenon they are studying. At the same time, designers, model builders, and inventors are involved in testing their drafts.

The fifth phase of the research process provides time for information researchers to organize and sequence their notes based on main ideas. At the same time, the experimenters and investigators are also busy organizing their work, but for these students, the organization involves their raw data. They have a decision to make: Does the analysis of these data allow them to accept or reject their hypotheses? Concurrently, the designers and inventors are busy sharing their prototypes and draft designs with others in order to gather feedback and make revisions.

During the last phase of the research process the inquiry questions are answered: orally, in writing, or through media. Rough drafts turn into final products, recommendations and findings are clarified, and often, the work is shared with an interested audience. More complete information about this phase is shared in Chapters 10 and 11.

Coaching Students to Use Research as a Stepping Stone for New Perspectives, Solutions, Products, Services, and Creativity

Once the research phase is completed, many students are interested in using their new knowledge or skills for specific purposes. These purposes usually incorporate the development of a product or service. Students involved in information research are likely to use their notes and findings to create a paper, video, or website that explains their findings. Investigative researchers are inclined to move from the data gathering phase to the development of a product that showcases their findings. Proposals, claims, and persuasive recommendations are likely to follow. Makers and designers move from the research phase to the development phase, explained in the next chapter. Their products might include plans, designs, prototypes, or models. In other cases, students might be interested in sharing their data with others and getting feedback from others who share their interests and concerns.

All good projects eventually come to an end. And with the end of a student's or small group's project and research comes the question, "What's next?" Assuming that your school or classroom has created a schedule that permits IBL projects and inquiries throughout the school year, we suggest that you consider integrating follow-up opportunities for students who want to extend their research work. Students who "catch" the research bug are likely to want to continue working within their interest area in some fashion. These junctures allow for extensions that allow us to reframe the original question and couple it with the research findings. With the help of a teacher-coach and willing peers, a brainstorming or fishbowl session might pose these questions to jumpstart the extension process:

- × How might we put this data or design to other uses?
- × How might we combine our worth with that of interested others?
- × Are there other problems and needs in my interest area that I could address?
- × Would a different communication vehicle for my research be useful or enjoyable?
- × Are there others who might find my research beneficial?
- × Who else might I interview, survey, or work with about my interest area?

Just as many professional writers keep a notebook, box, or drawer that contains potential ideas for future work, we recommend that students begin to keep a "Curiosity List." Whether it is stored on paper or digitally, this list becomes a strategy for noticing and recording ideas and questions that fascinate students. With proper coaching and support, these idle kernels have the potential to become future research projects.

Conclusion

This chapter provided you with an opportunity to think closely about the fifth phase of the IBL framework. We defined research and explained its purpose. We also demonstrated the numerous ways that IBL research aligns with national standards. Readers had the opportunity to compare three different categories of student research and their related processes. Lastly, we explored suggestions for extending students' IBL work with alternative research, products, and audiences. In Chapter 10, you will learn more about how the research phase assists students' product development.

CHAPTER 10

Developing Real-World Products

> The continual pursuit of connecting learning and the real world will only get more vital and intense. These various path to authenticity [e.g., authentic products, outcomes, equipment, skills, partners, problems, and audiences] can help solidify that connection.
>
> —Michael Niehoff

Identifying the most appropriate real-world products or outlets represents the sixth step in the IBL process. The best news is that students and teachers have already given some consideration to potential product formats or outlets. Not only were students asked if they had any ideas for product formats in My Action Planner (see Chapter 7), but also student and teacher conversations have surely broached the topic.

After reading this chapter, you will be able to:

1. define student products;
2. using a list of attributes, distinguish between traditional classroom products and the authentic product(s) of IBL;
3. brainstorm and select an appropriate real-world product or outlet for each student's/group of students' inquiry question;
4. identify and use six criteria to assess the most appropriate product format for each student's IBL project;
5. share the lists and criteria with students; and

6. if warranted, "backward map" each student's IBL topic and targeted product into current standards.

You may want to read the case study about Cullen either before reading or after reading this chapter (see Appendix A). His case study profiles a young man who did not complete an authentic product within the year's timeframe, but whose research earned him credit and pointed to a tangible and completed product in the next school year.

Traditional Classroom Products Versus Authentic Tasks, Products, and Performances

The final product is a critical component of the IBL project. Although there are smaller products along the way, such as the action plan, list of resources used, and journal prompts, the final product—usually a publicly presented product or performance—is the culmination of the student's work and is tangible evidence of student learning. These final products can be as simple as a one-pager or as complex as an iMovie or scientific experiment.

The culminating product in an IBL initiative is different from other, more traditional forms of classroom products, such as quizzes, worksheets, multiple-choice tests, book reports, and the like. The IBL product is distinguished from traditional classroom products by at least 10 attributes that are summarized in Table 10. There are marked differences between the more traditional types of classroom products and those that are considered authentic. How might you characterize the percentages of traditional and authentic products created by students in your school?

"Should all of my assessments be authentic?" you ask. "Absolutely not" is the answer; one type of product is not necessarily better than the other. There are times when traditional classroom products are more practical than the authentic ones. As the saying goes, "form follows function." In the final analysis, a students' portfolio of learning assignments will contain both traditional products and some that are more authentic. The variety of products should reflect the nature and purpose of the knowledge students are to acquire.

TABLE 10

Traditional Versus Authentic Classroom Products

Attribute	Traditional Products	IBL or Authentic Products
Purpose	Summative; to rank and compare students; assign a grade; to determine how well students have learned information	Formative; to measure student proficiency on real-world competencies, tasks, and product creation; to provide feedback to students so they can monitor and adjust their own learning progressions
Format	Usually a selected response; can have open-ended questions or essays	Usually produces a real-world task or performance
What it measures	Usually, declarative knowledge and skills	Applied learning, higher order thinking skills
Type of thinking required	Cognitive recall, sometimes analysis and synthesis	Construction of new meaning; use of higher order thinking skills, including creativity
Directness	Indirect measure; no evidence that learning can be applied	More direct measure; requires application of the knowledge and skills student(s) have acquired
Role of the student	Passive; lesson doer, test-taker	Student centered; students own their topic, the learning plan, learning sequence, and assessment
Role of the teacher	Evaluator	Facilitator, coach, managerial assistant
Time	Rigid and fixed, efficient	More flexible timelines decided upon by the students and teacher; time intensive
Relationship with instruction	Separate from instruction	Product or performance is part of instruction
Comprehensiveness	Snapshot	More comprehensive representation of what students know and are able to do

"I hate essays, but that's what I have done my whole school career. I want to be a preschool teacher, and I love creating lesson plans. When I had a chance to make a lesson plan that combined the best of Maria Montessori, I hugged myself in excitement. That was the most fun I had ever had in school."

—MADELYN, GRADE 7

Three Strategies for Selecting Authentic Products/ Performances/Outlets

For those students who want a real-world product, how do you help them select an appropriate format? There are hundreds of authentic formats used in the world every day. Do you simply pull an idea from the air? We do not expect practitioners or students to spend their time searching and selecting from the myriad real-world products and performances. Instead of starting from scratch, we suggest that you try three different strategies explained in this section. First, we list very common real-world formats in Table 11. These formats are frequently produced in real-world settings and are, at the same time, appropriate for both lower and upper elementary students.

Second, think back to the 16 career clusters that we mentioned in Chapter 5. For busy classroom teachers, we have created a list of cluster-specific products (see Appendix D). The list identifies real-world products that may be unique to each career cluster. It is aligned with upper elementary and middle school students (vs. lower elementary). Clearly, we know that there are more products aligned with the cluster than the 10 that are listed for each area. Thus, an editable version of the list is available on the book's webpage.

Third, consider that there are many notable real-world initiatives already underway that may align perfectly with a student's inquiry question. Specifically, some students may be able to "piggyback" on them. For example, Roots and Shoots (n.d.) is a well-established youth service program for young people of all ages. The mission of the organization is to "empower young people to affect positive change

TABLE 11
List of Real-World Products

Advertisement	Display	Puppet show
Bulletin board	Family Tree	Puzzle
Collage	Game	Questionnaire
Collection	Machine	Scrapbook
Computer program	Map	Sculpture
Costume	Mobile	Story
Demonstration	Model	Terrarium
Diagram	Musical composition	Toy
Diary	Painting	Trial
Dictionary	Photo mural	
Discussion	Play	

in their communities" (para. 1). Roots and Shoots has dozens of existing global programs underway. Further, the organization provides opportunities for students to design their own program and/or outlet for projects. Other notable organizations may prove useful, and readers may want to conduct their own online search for additional outlets that align with products students are creating. As with any digital platform used by children under 16, readers, educators, and/or their technology consultants should verify that the platform, service program, and/or sponsoring organization adheres to the federal COPPA (Children's Online Privacy Protection Act, 2000) laws and regulations.

With ideas from Table 11, Appendix D, and your online search in hand, you and your students are ready to consider selecting one or two of the most likely products or outlets for their IBL projects. Many times, students will come to you with an idea for a product format already in mind. Recall Andrea who wanted to investigate the latest features of iMovie. Early on, she identified that she wanted to create an iMovie, a very reasonable product choice in light of her research question. Pablo, concerned about the water quality in the river that flows through his neighborhood, decided he wanted to check the chemical composition and temperature of the river water north and south of the water treatment plant in town. Several product formats come to mind. He might conduct a research study and present the findings in a research paper. He could just as easily prepare a PowerPoint or Prezi presentation to be presented to the local town council. Further, if a local university is nearby and hosts a Young Scholars program, he might submit a proposal to present at the next scheduled conference.

Regardless of students' product choices, your guidance will be critical. Although students may come to you with a product format(s) they have already chosen, other students' products or outlets might not be as apparent. In your conferencing with each class member, you and your students will want to consider any and all of the following factors: (1) the student's age, experience, and maturity; (2) the nature of the inquiry question and investigation (e.g., scientific, historical, literary, or mathematical); (3) resources required (e.g., Internet connectivity, printing, mural space, etc.); (4) availability of facilities (i.e., if the culminating product is an oral presentation or a curated collection); (5) the availability of possible mentors; and (6) time sensitivity, if the final product is an entry into a conference, competition, or publishing outlet with a deadline.

Another Potential Opportunity to Backward Map Into Standards

Now that you have each student's IBL project and possible product identified, you have another opportunity to "backward map" into your standards if you have not done so already. "Don't give up the ship yet!" we exclaim. The task is much easier than you think. Most standards have, as a central focus, research and the application of content knowledge. Thus, practitioners need only review those standards that will most likely align directly with a student's topic and type of product.

What standards might Andrea address in her iMovie Project? The National Core Arts Standards contain anchor standards that are divided into four categories: creating, performing/presenting/producing, responding, and connecting (National Coalition for Core Arts Standards, 2015). In all likelihood, Andrea's iMovie would require that she address Anchor Standards 2, 3, 5, 6, 8, 9, 10, and 11.

How about Pablo and his research project into water quality in the river by his hometown? As an eighth grader, his IBL work falls squarely in the NGSS standard MS-ESS3-3: "Apply scientific principles to design a method for monitoring and minimizing a human impact on the environment" (NGSS Lead States, 2013). Additionally, his product would require him to address the scientific and engineering practices that are aligned to MS-ESS3.3.

Remember, too, that you do not teach in a vacuum. There are lots of other teachers in your building with expertise. If a student is doing a project outside your content area, pay a colleague the ultimate compliment by asking them the standards that will most likely align to the student's work. It's a win for you and a win for your trusted colleague.

Do not forget to identify the standards that align with each students' project on Resource 13: Project Tracker (p. 106). They will be a handy reference for anyone seeking to understand how your IBL initiative aligns with curriculum standards. We have provided you with space to list those on Resource 13.

Finally, note that some final products may not be aligned to the standards. Some student investigations may be, for example, a simple summary or set of working notes. In these cases, backward mapping will probably not prove reasonable or beneficial.

Conclusion

We covered a great deal of territory in this chapter on the products of an IBL initiative. Clearly, they are a cornerstone in the initiative because they enhance the "realness" of each student's project. In essence, they are one of the "acid tests" for what makes a problem real. We covered six weighty topics. We: (1) defined student products, (2) highlighted how IBL products differ from the more traditional classroom products, (3) offered two different strategies to jumpstart our thinking about potential real-world product formats, (4) provided six criteria by which teachers can support students' selection of real-world product formats, and (5) addressed several ways to link projects and products to standards.

What's next? You will turn your attention to real audiences. Who and what are they? How can you locate them in the community?

CHAPTER 11

Engaging Authentic Audiences

I can be a fire fighter and help everyone
Or baking like a baker sure would be fun
When I grow up I can be anything

—Mr. Rogers

A quotation by Mr. Rogers to open a chapter on the importance of authentic products in the classroom? We promise that the connection is a good one. Give us a few paragraphs to set the context and create the linkage.

This chapter address the significance of an authentic audience in an IBL project. Often, authentic products go hand-in-hand with authentic audiences. By the time you finish this chapter, you will have worked your way through the totality of the eight steps that we believe are critical to an interest-based learning initiative. As such, we hope that you now have a full vision of the process and recognize that the totality—and its impact on student learners—is greater than the sum of the individual parts.

Our vision would not be complete, however, if we did not address the topic of the authentic audience. What is an authentic audience? Why is an authentic audience an important component to an IBL project? How can you prepare your students for presenting in front of an authentic audience? How might you prepare authentic audience members? How do you begin to develop authentic audiences for students' projects? We will answer these questions in this chapter.

After reading this chapter, you will be able to:

1. define an authentic audience;
2. explain why authentic audiences can be important in interest-based learning initiatives, but not necessarily required;
3. use a set of questions to prepare those students who will present to an authentic audience (not all will or may want to);
4. understand how to best prepare authentic audience members;
5. describe at least five ways to begin developing an array of potential authentic audiences from the community and/or state.

What Is an Authentic Audience?

We often hear the term *authentic audience* used by educators. In fact, it has become a household term because our increasingly linked world has made connecting student-created content with others so easy. Because it has become a household term, we are not sure it means the same thing to everyone. An authentic audience is someone, or a small group of people, who already has a professional interest in your students or students' work. It is an audience that would choose to read or view the content. Authentic audiences are determined by the nature of the students' inquiry question, project, and findings. For example, if a student investigated the nutritional value of school cafeteria food, the audience might be the members of the board of education. If a student prepared notes about local legendary figures, the audience might be the local or state historical society. Likewise, if a small group of students created summaries about popular books, the audience might be the local librarians or an online group. Finally, if a student created some original comic strips, the audience might be local artists, journalists, or an online audience. The case studies in Appendix A reference noteworthy audiences for students' projects.

The Importance of an Authentic Audience

Do you remember *Mister Rogers' Neighborhood*, the PBS television show? Do you recollect his song "When I Grow Up I Can Be Anything"? For those of us who remember, the song is etched forever in our memories among his many other regular guests and sayings. For those of you who were born after his long-playing show, you will note that he has conspicuously enjoyed a resurgence of attention and affection because his voice is even more relevant and vital today. If you are new to Mr. Rogers, we have opened this chapter with some words from his song (see http://www.neighborhoodarchive.com/dtn/songs/when_grow_up_be_anything.html for the full lyrics).

The song reminds us that children have talents, abilities, and aspirations, and that educators need to see what sits invisibly behind each and every one of their faces. If you believe that your students have hidden talents and abilities, then it behooves you to act on those beliefs. You must provide them with opportunities to engage in real-world problems and offer ideas, solutions, and/or products that might benefit themselves or others. Interest-based learning provides practitioners with a unique opportunity to "love children into being," by providing them with opportunities to engage with learning on their terms, offer their ideas and solutions, and showcase their work to an authentic audience. These opportunities ought *not* to occur after a student graduates (i.e., when they are "grown up"), but iteratively across the K–12 learning span. Otherwise, you risk overlooking and underrealizing students' abilities.

You need to provide your young people with opportunities to set personal goals, take ownership in their learning program, reflect accurately upon their learning progress and adjust accordingly, and make an impact. They are capable of and need the opportunity to make an impact on the wider community.

"You mean *every* student?" you ask quizzically. "Yes and no," is our answer. Every student should have the opportunity to present their work to an authentic audience. But not all students may want to present in such a fashion. They may not have a product that is ready for showcasing. Furthermore, they may not yet be willing to take on the additional challenges that the presentation entails.

What Is the Rationale for Authentic Audiences?

There are a number of significant reasons for providing students with the opportunity to present their work to an authentic audience. We have noted patterns in students' behaviors when they realize that practitioners from the community or online will view/hear their work. That recognition:

1. **changes the focus of learning:** Instead of focusing on meeting a teachers' standards and/or expectations, students involved with an authentic audience tend to focus more on the process and overall quality of the end product.

2. **holds the power to be transformative:** Students who realize the significance of an authentic audience, come to see themselves as creators whose work has value in the world outside of school. For many young people, this is a new identity that can be transformative.

3. **increases student purpose and motivation:** Students have shared many reflections with us as they pursue personally meaningful topics that will be shared with the wider community. Some have shared that when they have to communicate to someone other than the teacher or classmates, it makes them think "more precisely," make "better and more clear connections across content areas and topics," and learn "more" than they would have with a regular school project.

4. **may drive additional learning:** As practitioners, we have witnessed hundreds of students sharing their work with professionals or community members. In the vast majority of the cases, audience members asked pertinent and perceptive questions; offered opinions; provided student presenters with genuine, professional, and positive reflection on specific aspects of the work; suggested additional resources or avenues to pursue; and/or offered tangential questions for possible related research. Put simply, authentic audiences drove the cycle of purposeful student learning.

5. **requires a different lens:** When students create classroom work, they often view it through the lens of the teacher or, perhaps, a rubric. When young people operate with the knowledge that they will present their project to authentic members of a given field, they begin to see their content and work progress through the eyes of their newly defined audience members.

For readers wanting to learn more about the power of authentic audiences in the classroom, please see Levy (2008).

We believe that authentic audiences can help to stop the loss of student momentum on class work. Further, we believe we need to change the traditional paradigm, and you have a small opportunity to do this through IBL initiatives and the strategic use of authentic audiences. Instead of saying, "Turn it in," you need to be saying, for example, "Present it to the community, "Showcase your art work," and "Publish it online."

How to Prepare Students for Presentations to Real Audiences

"But," you exclaim, "my students have never presented in front of authentic audiences! At best, their work has gone to me and/or other fellow students. How am I supposed to get them ready for this experience? The last thing I want to do is set them up!"

Without question, we believe you must prepare students to address real audiences. Our field experiences suggest you can share with students the following list of questions. You can have students think about and write down some possible answers that you can discuss in a brief conference. Or, if you rather, you can conduct a longer conference and, in a back-and-forth manner, pose and develop answers to each of the questions.

1. Who are the members of my real audience?
2. What are the big ideas that govern the field?
3. What are routine problems/issues in the field?
4. What skills do the practitioners in the field use to solve problems?
5. How might they draw conclusions?
6. What are the hallmarks of quality work in the field?
7. What is my "ask" of them (e.g., their reactions/suggestions, next research questions, other related resources, introductions to others in the field)?

It goes without saying that your work ahead of time with students will not only prepare them, but also allay any anxiety they may have. Never once in all of our collective years did we witness any authentic audience member be callous, insensitive, inappropriate, or less-than-complimentary to the young person presenting.

> "I ended up completing an oral presentation on my passion: an analysis of the interrelated themes in Tyler the Creator's album 'Flower Boy.' When I finished my presentation to my audience, I turned to my teacher, one of the audience members, and said: 'I can't believe this. I am so sorry. I talked for over an hour!'"
>
> **—BEATRICE, GRADE 8**

How to Prepare Authentic Audience Members

Just as you prepare your students, so too can you prepare your targeted audience members if they come from the community or state. In all likelihood, you will establish preliminary contact by phone to extend an invitation to the presentation. In all likelihood, too, you will follow up the oral invitation with a brief letter that contains the particulars related to the date, time, and place. We suggest that you include a brief summary or abstract of the student's IBL project. This way, your audience members can be thinking ahead about the content, related references they might know, etc.

Creating an Ongoing Catalog of Authentic Audiences for IBL Projects

Locating authentic audiences for your students' IBL projects is crucial. Here are some tips to help you get started with potential local and/or state audience members:

× **familiar people:** The nature of the project students complete naturally will influence the audience membership. After students create a research question and have an idea about a potential product, have each student think about who—in the community or state—might already have a vested interest in the work. For example, one entire class involved with IBL recently held a celebration for students' extended families to interact with student creations, such as displays of interviews for an ancestry project. One of the most powerful audiences was a group of World War II veterans who were invited to be part of the opening ceremonies for two young men's World War II museum that contained artifacts collected from members of the community.

× **notable locals:** Think about the members of your community who can spare a half-day visit to your school: Selectmen and -women, police personnel, board of education members, local business owners, state department workers, clergy members, and local university personnel are only a few of the local people who usually are flattered to be asked to be part of students' research and members of an authentic audience to hear the results of students' investigations. Note that these people will need to be provided with plenty of time to get the event on their frequently overbooked calendars.

× **cold calls:** In todays' 24/7 connected world, it is easier than ever before to reach out to individuals via Gmail or a text. This method works well for inviting local people to be members of an audience and/or a resource to support a project that is underway. For example, primary grade students working on a project on ecosystems could share their questions/products with a local or state zoologist via a 30-minute virtual visit by videophone. It is relatively simple to look on the website of the person's organization for contact information.

× **tweet your requests:** Are you as amazed as we are with the power of Twitter? With Twitter, you can send out a message to your network asking for support or send a tweet to an expert who would make a great audience for your students. If you're not a Twitter user, you might post a request to friends and family on Facebook to see if someone can help in the research process or be an audience participant.

With so many things to be juggling during an IBL initiative, we suggest that you begin to keep a running list of contacts. Across your years with IBL learning initiatives, your organization and tracking will prove an invaluable time saver.

Gathering Acceptable Global Audiences

Powerful interaction with real audiences is no longer limited to the state or local community. In the 21st century, students can now showcase their work to limitless global audiences. We suggest that readers look into the use of G Suite for Education by Google because it is already in use in many schools across the country. G Suite contains Gmail and Google Classroom, Drive, Calendar, Vault, Docs, Sheets, Forms, Slides, Sites, and Hangouts. The G Suite apps are free to schools, although add-ons may carry fees. For the purposes here, G Suite supports collaboration among students, faculty, and parents. As such, it is a practical, accessible vehicle for supporting authentic audiences for students' IBL learning.

Beyond G Suite, there are hundreds of other online platforms that showcase student work, and they are usually product specific, such as for essays, stories, videos, and other types of artwork. Interested readers can locate them within seconds by searching online.

"Carl and Malik really like skateboards too, so they said they are gonna be in the group that wants to see my project."

—EDDIE, GRADE 2

CASE STUDIES
Andrea and Pablo

The audiences for Andrea's and Pablo's IBL dictated themselves, so to speak. Andrea chose to complete a stop motion animation iMovie to showcase interviews with middle schoolers (her peers who volunteered) in a documentary called *Middle School Madness*. Her goal was to illuminate for the school's faculty the perspectives of its students as they navigated the difficulties of adolescence and middle school. She liked being able to stop the action of the movie to edit in interview clips with actual students.

Pablo conducted his research, wrote up his findings, and presented his research in a Prezi format to treatment plant officials and the town council. Many accolades came his way from interested citizens and town officials.

Conclusion

You should now clearly see the logical connection between authentic products and authentic audiences. They go hand-in-hand. As you conclude this section, you should be able to: (1) define what an authentic audience is, (2) explain why they are critical to students in today's classrooms, (3) explain how to prepare both young people and authentic audience members for an IBL presentation, (4) name several ways to jumpstart an ongoing list of local and state personnel who might participate as authentic audience members, and (5) identify online platforms that can be used to showcase student work.

CHAPTER 12

Reflecting, Debriefing, and Celebrating

The more you praise and celebrate your life, the more there is to celebrate.

—Oprah Winfrey

Study without reflection is a waste of time; reflection without study is dangerous.

—Confucius

You are nearing the end of the IBL process. With that thought in mind, however, we have a couple of things yet to do, but they are the easiest of the tasks that we have outlined so far. This chapter will address debriefing, a rational for its use, a set of debriefing questions, and, finally, talk about the importance of celebrations along the journey.

After reading this chapter, you will be able to:
1. define debriefing,
2. explain a rationale for its use,
3. analyze and use a set of debriefing questions, and
4. provide examples of celebrations practitioners can use to celebrate small and large accomplishments in an IBL initiative.

Debriefing

Debriefing is a reflective technique used to gauge how successful, useful, and/or beneficial a learning journey was and to discern what could have made the journey better for key constituents. It is based on the premise that for students to learn, they must make time for reflection. Unfortunately, reflection is a step that is often overlooked, whether it is the world of business or education. Regardless of context, it is one of the most important steps in a learning journey because it solidifies learning and takes it to the "next step."

Debriefing can be used for a variety of reasons beyond assessing the nature of a learning journey. These reasons can include honing critical thinking skills, fostering lifelong learning mindsets, analyzing and pinpointing areas for improvement, and increasing self-knowledge. In many ways, reflection is also a building block of metacognitive strategies, a major component of social-emotional learning.

The most effective debriefings are structured. Structure does not mean scripted, however. One way to structure debriefing questions is to divide them into three categories: The What, So What, and Now What questions (Senge, 1990). The following questions, arranged in the three aforementioned categories, can be used anywhere along the learning journey with IBL: after each stage of the process; after a particularly turbulent, confusing, successful or exciting IBL event; or as closure midway or at the conclusion of the process.

The What questions are designed to elicit the observations and perceptions of participants. Examples include:

- What happened?
- What did you expect?
- What was your reaction?
- What is your recollection of the sequence of events?
- What did you observe?
- What roles did you play?
- What were the roles of others?
- What was challenging about _____ ?
- What was easy about _____ ?
- What were some of your most powerful learning moments?
- When did you realize that you had come up with your best solution?
- What was your biggest problem, and how did you solve it?
- How did you gauge your progress?
- What were your milestones?
- What did you discover were your greatest strengths . . . greatest challenges?

Reflecting, Debriefing, and Celebrating

The So What questions are designed to look at the details of the learning and draw out the significance and consequences of the experience so that insights can be generated. Examples include, but are not limited to:

× What did you expect to learn from _____ ?
× What new learning did you actually take away from _____ ?
× What surprised you?
× How has your perspective about _____ changed?
× What made the challenging situations so demanding?
× What made the easy situations so effortless?
× How might you prioritize your new learning?

The Now What questions act as bridges. They connect the significance or impact generated in the So What questions to future experiences. As such, they are designed to get participants thinking ahead so that they can apply their new learning. These bridging questions include, for example:

× How can you apply your new learning?
× What would you like to learn more about?
× What follow-up should we provide based upon any challenges or difficulties you faced?
× If you did the project again, what would you do differently?

Debriefings do not have to be long and involved. What is most important to remember is to conduct them regularly. They can help refine your work with IBL. When you model these strategies, you teach your students invaluable critical, meta-cognitive, and lifelong learning skills and habits.

> "It is important to understand that the teacher has just as much to learn from the students as we have to learn from the teachers. If the teacher allows students to conduct independent research, she or he creates personal excitement in her students. Ultimately, she may learn even more about her students."
>
> **—WESTLY, GRADE 5**

Celebrations

Have you ever felt like you were on a treadmill? Have you ever wished that you could slow down and configure a more meaningful and joyful way to teach and live? We're pretty sure that you will shout out a loud and emphatic "YES," just like we do.

We have friends in a business firm, and they never miss an opportunity to revel when each job is completed. They might go out for coffee, pop a bottle of champagne, or treat themselves to a movie. Their ritual allows them to stop the treadmill—even for a short while—to honor and talk about their accomplishments.

What we are about to suggest is that we must stop the treadmill more often in our classrooms, especially during an IBL initiative. It is essential to celebrate not just major accomplishments, but also the small ones. In the context of IBL that might translate into everyone in the class having an interest topic identified, sharing their research or products, or completion of several students' oral presentations, just to name a few.

The reason? When we get into a productivity mode, it is too easy to let accomplishments slide. The result is that important milestones fade away. With that said, we are clearly mindful of time constraints, every teacher's biggest competitor. We are convinced, however, that with judicious planning, we can bring a better balance to productivity in the classroom and the celebrations that should punctuate achievements.

Conclusion

After reading the short pages in this chapter, you will have a better sense of the debriefing process and the importance of celebrations. Specifically, you should be able to define debriefing, explain a rationale for its use, use a set of debriefing questions, and be better able to balance productivity in the classroom with important celebrations.

Additionally, it is important here to bring a conclusion to this guidebook. We began and will end with the same premise. Interest-based learning is a manageable process and curriculum catalyst. We have hopefully illuminated the steps of the process so that they are clear, understandable, and very doable. Equally important, the steps we articulated are universal and foundational; they transfer across the varied interest-based initiatives, including Genius Hour, passion projects, and Makerspaces, just to name a few. We hope the universality of our process makes teachers' jobs and choices easier.

Reflecting, Debriefing, and Celebrating

Additionally, we have also built the case for the transformative power of interest-based learning. By providing young people with more of a voice, honoring their interests for a small portion of classroom time, and becoming a facilitator of students' visions for themselves, you can transform your classroom. By doing so, we hope that your learners become more engaged, satisfied, purposeful, and connected to the future that is at their doorstep.

IBL is deeply rooted in the belief that all learners deserve the opportunity to construct meaning about themselves not only as consumers of knowledge, but also as producers of knowledge. The 21st century is here, and every mind needs to be engaged and productive, ready to not only consume the fire hydrant of knowledge at their fingertips, but also produce and create.

Does IBL fit into the vision for excellent classrooms? We sure hope so. For the purposes of this guidebook, we define excellent classrooms as places that purposefully foster and extend each individual's reach and possibilities, teachers and students alike.

We hope the case has been convincing for you. We hope that you try out our suggestions, adapt them, and refine them, all while honing your own skills. In the end, we hope you—like the students you serve and those who are described in this book—construct your own meaning, connections, reflections, and celebrations, and thereby reach even higher levels of professional expertise.

REFERENCES

Advance CTE. (n.d.). *Career clusters.* https://careertech.org/career-clusters

Alexander, J. M., Johnson, K. E., Leibham, M. E., & Kelley, K. (2008). The development of conceptual interests in young children. *Cognitive Development, 23*(2), 324–334. https://doi.org/10.1016/j.cogdev.2007.11.004

Children's Online Privacy Protection Act of 1998, 15 U.S.C. 6501–6505 (1998). https://www.ftc.gov/enforcement/rules/rulemaking-regulatory-reform-proceedings/childrens-online-privacy-protection-rule

Coiro, J. (2014). *Teaching adolescents how to evaluate the quality of online information.* Edutopia. https://www.edutopia.org/blog/evaluating-quality-of-online-info-julie-coiro

Colangelo, N., Assouline, S. G., & Gross, M. U. M. (Eds.). (2004). *A nation deceived: How schools hold back America's brightest students* (Vol. 2). The University of Iowa, The Connie Belin & Jacqueline N. Blank International Center for Gifted Education and Talent Development.

Csikszentmihalyi, M. (1990). *Flow: The psychology of optimal experience.* Harper and Row.

Deci, E. L., & Ryan, R. M. (1985). *Intrinsic motivation and self-determination in human behavior.* Plenum Press.

Dewey, J. (1913). *Interest and effort in education.* Houghton Mifflin.

Dewey, J. (1938). *Experience and education.* Macmillan.

Education Commission of the States. (1994). *Prisoners of time.* Author.

Frey, N., Fisher, D., & Smith, D. (2019). *All learning is social and emotional: Helping students develop essential skills for the classroom and beyond.* ASCD.

Fullan, M., Gardner M., & Drummy, M. (2019). Going deeper. *Educational Leadership, 76*(8), 64–69.

Harackiewicz, J., Durik, A., Barron, K., Linnenbrink-Garcia, L., & Tauer, J. (2008). The role of achievement goals in the development of interest: Reciprocal relations between achievement goals, interest, and performance. *Journal of Educational Psychology, 100*(1), 105–122. https://doi.org/10.1037/0022-0663.100.1.105

Hattie, J. (2009). *Visible learning: A synthesis of over 800 meta-analyses relating to achievement.* Routledge.

Hattie, J. (2012). *Visible learning for teachers: Maximizing impact on learning.* Routledge.

Hidi, S. (2006). Interest: A unique motivational variable. *Educational Research Review, 1*(2), 69–82. https://doi.org/10.1016/j.edurev.2006.09.001

Hidi, S., & Renninger K. A. (2006). The four-phase model of interest development. *Educational Psychologist, 41*(2), 111–127. https://doi.org/10.1207/s15326985ep4102_4

Hunter, M. C. (1982). *Mastery teaching: Increasing instructional effectiveness in elementary, and secondary schools, colleges and universities.* TIP Publishers.

Iyengar, S. S., & Lepper, M. R. (2000). When choice is demotivating: Can one desire too much of a good thing? *Journal of Personality and Social Psychology, 79*(6), 995–1,006. https://doi.org/10.1037/0022-3514.79.6.995

Kirkpatrick, W. H. (1918). *The project method: The use of the purposeful act in the educative process.* Teacher's College, Columbia University.

Lancelot, W. H. (1944). *Permanent learning: A study in educational techniques.* Wiley & Sons.

Levy, S. (2008). The power of audience. *Educational Leadership, 66*(3), 75–79.

Martinez, S. L., & Stager, G. S. (2013). *Invent to learn: Making, tinkering, and engineering in the classroom.* Constructing Modern Knowledge Press.

Moss, C. M., & Brookhart, S. M. (2019). *Advancing formative assessment in every classroom: A guide for instructional leaders* (2nd ed.). ASCD.

National Coalition for Core Arts Standards. (2015). *National Core Art Standards.* https://www.nationalartsstandards.org

National Council for the Social Studies. (2013). *The College, Career, and Civic Life (C3) Framework for Social Studies State Standards: Guidance for enhancing the rigor of K–12 civics, economics, geography, and history.* https://www.socialstudies.org/c3

National Governors Association Center for Best Practices, & Council of Chief State School Officers. (2010a). *Common Core State Standards for English language arts.* http://www.corestandards.org/ELA-Literacy

National Governors Association Center for Best Practices, & Council of Chief State School Officers. (2010b). *Common Core State Standards for mathematics.* http://www.corestandards.org/Math

Newmann, F. M., & Wehlage, G. G. (1995). *Successful school restructuring: A report to the public and educators.* Center on Organization and Restructuring of Schools.

NGSS Lead States. (2013). *Next generation science standards: For states, by states.* The National Academies Press.

Partnership for 21st Century Learning. (2019). *Framework for 21st century learning.* http://static.battelleforkids.org/documents/p21/P21_Framework_Brief.pdf

Patall, E. A., Cooper, H., & Robinson, J. C. (2008).The effects of choice on intrinsic motivation and related outcomes: A meta-analysis of research findings. *Psychological Bulletin, 134*(2), 270–300. https://doi.org/10.1037/0033-2909.134.2.270

Patall, E. A., Cooper, H., & Wynn, S. R. (2010). The effectiveness and relative importance of choice in the classroom. *Journal of Educational Psychology, 102*(4), 896–915. https://doi.org/10.1037/a0019545

Pilgrim, J., Vasinda, S., Bledsoe, C., & Martinez, E. (2019). Critical thinking is critical: Octopuses, online sources, and reliability reasoning. *The Reading Teacher, 73*(1), 85–93. https://doi.org/10.1002/trtr.1800

Renzulli, J. S. (1982). What makes a problem real: Stalking the illusive meaning of qualitative differences in gifted education. *Gifted Child Quarterly, 26*(4), 147–156. https://doi.org/10.1177/001698628202600401

Rogers, K., & Kimpston, R. (1992). The acceleration of students: What we know vs what we do. *Educational Leadership, 50*(2), 58–61.

Roots and Shoots. (n.d.). *About.* https://www.rootsandshoots.org

Schaar, J. H. (1981). *Legitimacy in the modern state.* Transaction.

Schiefele, U., & Csikszentmihalyi, M. (1995). Motivation and ability as factors in mathematics experience and achievement. *Journal for Research in Mathematics Education, 26*(2), 163–181. https://doi.org/10.2307/749208

Senge, P. M. (1990). *The fifth discipline: The art and practice of the learning organization.* Doubleday.

Tomlinson, C. A., Brighton, C., Hertberg, H., Callahan, C. M., Moon, T. R., Brimijoin, K., & Reynolds, T. (1998). Differentiating instruction in response to student readiness, interest, and learning profile in academically diverse classrooms: A review of literature. *Journal for the Education of the Gifted, 27*(2/3), 119–145. https://doi.org/10.1177/016235320302700203

Tomlinson, C. A., & Jarvis, J. (2006). Teaching beyond the book. *Teaching to Student Strengths, 64*(1), 16–21.

Vygotsky, L. S. (1978). *Mind in society.* Harvard University Press.

Wiggins, G. (1994). Reporting what students are learning. *Educational Leadership, 52*(2), 28.

Wiggins, G., & McTighe, J. (1998). *Understanding by design.* ASCD.

Wineburg, S., McGrew, S., Breakstone, J., & Ortega, T. (2016). *Evaluating information: The cornerstone of civic online reasoning.* Stanford Digital Repository. http://purl.stanford.edu/fv751yt5934

APPENDIX A

Case Studies

Jared, Grade 8
(Student With Learning Disability)

Jared entered my eighth-grade class as a new student who had been home-schooled since grade 5. Responding to the bullying of their son in elementary school in a different district, his parents had removed him from that system and chose to school him at home. Upon moving to our district 3 years later, they opted to give the public school system a chance, once again.

He was track runner, very quiet to the point of introversion, and had little understanding of the formal structures in the public education system. Often, when I assigned whole-class independent work after mini-lessons, Jared would go off task, move to the back of the room, and read silently. His general background knowledge had gaps, and socially he was awkward.

He was never disruptive or disrespectful. When redirected, he would politely say, "thank you," and return to the class assignment. It appeared hard to keep this young man focused. Additionally, his skill set was so limited that he frequently had trouble expressing himself coherently in writing and speaking. He needed enormous amounts of scaffolding to comprehend grade-level texts.

I knew that he would be one of my "high-mileage" kids when it came to interest-based learning; I would need to provide him with significant amounts of differentiation and scaffolding. Initially, he decided to write a personal narrative, but the work fell flat. He was unable to develop realistic narratives about himself. As an alternative, we worked off his interest in the online game *Fortnite*. He realized he could create narratives around the campaigns he was running in the game. Ultimately, and after many tries, he could not create a logical order to his storylines. He struggled with time, tense, and chronology. I realized that he needed much more structure and support than I could give him in the regular classroom.

I liked Jared a great deal, and I wanted to see him successful and to see him be able to finish some type of product. I made a referral to the middle school specialist, my coteacher who handled students who were unable to manage the regular classroom setting. She provided scaffolding for Jared in many ways, including with initiation, focusing supports, and class transitions.

Eventually, he finished a narrative. It was not to grade-level standards, but his learning curve had been enormous. There was much yet to do to polish the narrative, and my coteacher ended the year indicating that she would connect with the grade 9 teachers and special education staff at the high school at the start of the next school year.

Tyreke, Grade 6
(Advanced Learner, Eager Beaver, High Level of Topic Expertise)

Tyreke was overwhelmed. He had never had an opportunity to study the Civil Rights Movement outside of Dr Martin Luther King, Jr., and Malcolm X, and I had had recently told him to look into Rep. John Lewis after seeing him speak down in Alexandria, VA. Not even 2 days later, Tyreke was at my door. He had a list of more than 10 civil rights leaders and had taken a plethora of notes on several of them. He exclaimed that he had spent the last 2 days glued to his computer: "Just when I thought I had a good list," Tyreke said, "another civil rights leader surfaced!" I realized that this young man was on a roll and that I would not be able to keep up with him. That terrified me because much of what he was doing was outside of my comfort zone as a White, male teacher. I had studied the Civil Rights Movement and had even gone deeper with studies in African American literature as well as race and ethnic relations, but here was a young Black man developing his identity right in front of me. Did I have sufficient personal experience with or connection to this topic? How could I possibly help him?

That night I realized something. It was okay for Tyreke to be moving at 100 miles an hour. His passion was exhilarating for me to watch and contagious. *And* it was okay that he was already more knowledgeable than I was about the topic. My job was to facilitate his work, not to be as knowledgeable as he was about his chosen topic. In a school with a number of diverse cultures without necessarily having a significant population of African American students, he had an authentic audience to inform regarding the Civil Rights Movement and its leaders. My goals were to (1) connect him with John Lewis to determine if he might be interested in talking to Tyreke and (2) figure out how Tyreke could present his information. I had been thinking about a series of profiles during the month of February, Black History month, to accompany the morning announcements.

But I was way down the road! The first thing I had to do with Tyreke was to slow him down a tad and help him be more planful and systematic. He certainly did not need support finding his interest area! With that said, I knew I needed to conference with him very soon regarding his action plan, My Action Plan (MAP). Collaboratively, we needed to map out his goals, his next five steps with dates to be accomplished, and identify his resources.

In the end, Tyreke's project was one that teachers dream about. He presented six of his written portraits proudly over the intercom in February. He was a school celebrity!

I was not concerned about Tyreke's final product. I was confident that his voluminous research notes, as well as the quality of his work, were sufficient for any assessment protocol. His increased self-awareness was remarkable.

Needless to say, Tyreke wanted to continue with his work well beyond the end of the school year. I spoke with the seventh-grade language arts teacher and let her know about this work and passion of this unique young man.

Small Group of Girls, Grade 8
(Issues With Group Dynamics)

Tiffany was upset and stopped talking because her best friends were not listening. Tiffany, Aliyah, Kinzey, Katherine, and Alison had been close friends since elementary school. They did most things together, and, despite frequent disagreements, the girls were usually able to work out their differences. They each faced significant social issues as they completed their last year in middle school. Aliyah was African American, and completely separate from the Somali refugee population that comprised 30% of the student body that identified primarily as African refugees; Alison suffered from anxiety stemming from unstable home issues; Olivia struggled with body image; Tiffany also had body image issues related to a medical condition that stunted her growth; and Kinzey struggled with gender identity.

Their current disagreement concerned the focus of their interest-based learning project. Although the five expressed unbridled excitement at the thought that they could work collaboratively as a small group on a project of their choice, the excitement quickly vanished as they tried to decide on a single focus for their small-group work. Each of the girls wanted the focus of the project to be on their issue, whether it be prejudice, stress and anxiety, body image, or gender identity.

How could I support the passion that this group generated and still honor each of these unique young women? During a conference with the group, I posed a pivotal, leading question: How are these issues connected? In the subsequent conversation I facilitated with the girls, they realized that each of the individual issues fit under a much larger umbrella: social issues faced by young women in middle school. I could see the excitement begin to rekindle in the eyes of these young ladies. "Wow!" said Katherine.

By asking the question "How can we present these five unique stories that had a common thread?" we were able to move forward in the creative process. The girls gushed with ideas. "We could do a series of short stories!" Tiffany exclaimed. "Could we do them through digital storytelling?" Alison asked tentatively. All of us looked at her, stunned because we realized that she had come up with the solution.

I arranged a meeting with a colleague of mine, Joel Blackwell, who was running a digital storytelling club, and the students were delighted to take charge and lead the meeting. They explained what they wanted to do and shared with him some of their ideas. Joel provided the students with storyboard templates and other resources so that they could move forward relatively independently on their respective projects. He even offered to be a mentor and invited them to become members of the Digital Storytelling Club.

I watched the small group work diligently on their respective pieces. They exuded an earnestness in their mission to change aspects of the school. As I watched these young women, I was already thinking about an appropriate real-world audience for their work. Clearly, it went beyond their classmates. I shared the emerging projects with my principal and asked her about the feasibility of presenting the short projects to staff members toward the end of the year, when I knew the students would be ready. She got back to me after speaking with our building vice principal. They both agreed that the presentation would not only showcase the students' fine work, but also illuminate some areas for needed change in the school. We scheduled the presentation for mid-June.

My students were wide-eyed when I share the news with them about their end-of-the-year presentation with the building staff. "Us? That's scary!" they all chimed in at once. They were not sure they were up to the pressure of the task. I told them that together we could "face their fears," and that if they were serious about trying to change things at the school, that the staff and building administrators were the most appropriate audience to enact the kinds of changes that they desired. I added that I would support them with practice sessions and provide them with a series of questions that would help them better address their target audience.

This group's story has a happy ending. I was able to allay the students' fears by helping them understand that if they were serious about their work, they would be taken seriously by an adult audience. Further, the practice sessions were enormously helpful, the questions that I used to help prepare them to understand the nuances of a real-world audience were effective, and their final presentations were well-received. Administration and teachers thanked the students for their work, and my principal and vice principal reported that they were committed to looking into the issues illuminated in each girl's vignette. Additionally, my building-level administrators approached me at the conclusion of the presentation and shared that they were impressed with the quality, depth, creativity and sincerity of the students' work.

Cullen, Grade 7
(Lots of Interests, Many of Them Fleeting)

Cullen was a seventh grader, bigger than his peers and often disruptive in class. He had little impulse control, yet had a remarkable repertoire of knowledge about a wide range of topics, well beyond his peers. He was particularly fascinated by military history with an intense focus on World War II. When I introduced the whole notion of interest-based learning to the class in October, he was one of the students who stood out in my mind. I knew that the open-ended opportunity would appeal to him. However, I also had some genuine concerns. How do I support this young man with his anger management issues while other students in the class are working on their respective projects? I knew I would need to give him as much freedom as possible. Yet, at the same time, I would need to monitor his progress and moods closely. I worried how he would respond to my constructive criticism on his work, on the overall quality and complexity of his progress, and how he would react when I had to impose standards-based frameworks on his learning growth.

At the outset, he could not settle on a project topic because his range of interests was so wide. He began with the Roman invasion of England in 54 AD, then went to the Napoleonic wars, and then to the American Revolution. Each time he changed his topic, we began discussions about what his goal might be with each iteration. Before anything concrete was finalized in his action plan (MAP), he changed his mind again. The turning point arrived mid-winter when his social studies class began studying World War II. One day he came running in and showed me a list of books he had compiled on the war. They ranged from *The Diary of Anne Frank* to *Band of Brothers.* I sensed his overpowering interest, as well as the scope and range of information available, and knew that this was a topic that would sustain a long-term project.

Looking back, I was pleased that I allowed Cullen the time to flit from one topic to another at the outset of the year. I must admit that his flitting had made me nervous because I feared he would never settle. In fact, he was one of the last students to finalize an idea. But my waiting paid off handsomely because Cullen was now genuinely hooked on a topic that he alone had chosen and now owned.

My other worry point with Cullen was that there was no prospect of a finished product by the end of the year. I realized that this was not as important as I once thought because I could easily demonstrate his learning growth through his research notes, my conference notes with him, his journal prompt responses, and his book talks with me.

Fatima, Grade 6
(Issues With Self-Initiation)

Fatima was a sixth grader who had trouble buying into most class work. Her older sister was highly motivated, and Fatima never felt that she got out from under her sister's shadow. Once engaged, especially in an area of interest, however, she was able to work reasonably independently.

I knew from the outset that, although the interest-based learning project would be a good entry point for her, the open ended nature of the project would present challenges for her. I envisioned three hurdles—common to many students—that we would have to overcome: (1) project initiation, including interest finding and focusing; (2) project development, including product identification and targeting an audience; and (3) revising her work based on constructive feedback.

My first steps with Fatima were critical. Most importantly, I knew I had to assure her that the choice of project topic would be hers alone. After the large-group vision-making session, I floated throughout the classroom, answering questions. Fatima raised her hand and, when I approached her, she said softly, "I heard some other students talking with you about their projects with music. Can I do something like that?"

I reflected back what I heard her asking. "So, you want to do something related to lyrical analysis, specifically with hip-hop?" I asked. "That would be a great idea, Fatima! What I need from you will be an inquiry question and how your work will align with our language arts curriculum. How about we split those two tasks?"

I went on, "Your friends are researching where lyrics come from and how they relate to their chosen artist's life/lives. Would your inquiry question be similar?" Fatima nodded. I continued, "So, here's what I need from you. Tonight, could you write down your question, identify three to five songs that you would like to study, and print them out for me? I will work on the second task, which is to research the crosswalk between your lyric analysis and our language arts curriculum."

I realized how important that "over-the-shoulder" moment had been to Fatima. By conferencing with her for just a minute or two, I was hopeful that I had unleashed her engagement with an idea. I also realized how important it was to follow up with her as quickly and, more importantly, as thoroughly as possible so that she did not stall out and collapse on her idea.

For the moment, I was pleased with Fatima's progress and engagement, and I looked forward to touching base with her over the next couple of days regarding her progress. Although I knew there would be other hurdles ahead for this young woman and her interest-based learning project, we had made a good start that both of us were comfortable with.

APPENDIX B

Background Research and Theories

The research that is most aligned with interest-based learning is outlined in this section. We begin with a brief review of three foundational educational theories upon which IBL is based: social development theory (Vygotsky, 1978), self-determination theory (Deci & Ryan, 1985), and the theory of optimal learning environments (Csikszentmihalyi, 1990). We provide a brief description of each and discuss how to integrate the three theories into IBL. Finally, we provide recent and empirical research related to the use of classroom choice.

Note that this section does not list the hundreds of articles/books/blogs about choice. Although they are significant, they do not empirically support the use of choice with students in the classroom and, thus, do not provide the defensibility that practitioners need when they approach their administrators or other audiences for approval to implement IBL during classroom time.

Also note that Hattie's work is not listed here. His well-respected meta-analyses related to student achievement in the classroom (Hattie, 2012) did not indicate a significant effect size for choice because his singular independent variable was student achievement. He did not analyze other important independent variables, such as motivation, time on task, overall quality of student work, etc.

Social Development Theory

A major theme of Vygotsky's (1978) social development theory is that social interaction plays a primary role in the development of cognition. Vygotsky is, perhaps, best known for introducing the term *zone of proximal development* (ZPD). ZPD is the difference between what a learner can do without help and what they cannot do. Vygotsky believed that the role of education was to provide students with ongoing learning opportunities that are within students' ZPD, not too difficult to be mastered without peer or teacher guidance and not too easy. Optimum learning occurs when students operate continually within their ZPD.

Self-Determination Theory

Self-determination theory (SDT) is a theory of motivation, and it was developed by Deci and Ryan (1985) almost 40 years ago. Self-determination theory focuses primarily on internal sources of motivation, such as a need to gain knowledge or independence, now known as intrinsic motivation (vs. extrinsic motivation). To become self-determined, people—and students—need to feel:

×   Competent: Mastery of tasks and different skills.
×   Connected: A sense of belonging and attachment to other people.
×   Autonomous: In control of their own behaviors and goals.

Many current theorists now contend that making choices and asserting preferences is a key component to self-determination. Applied to the educational context, when students learn to make choices, they take control over their learning and actions. By taking ownership of their learning, we believe they become more intrinsically motivated, will persist longer at tasks, and, hopefully, learn more.

Optimal Learning Environments

In his seminal work, *Flow: The Psychology of Optimal Experience*, Csikszentmihalyi (1990) outlined his Flow theory, or positive psychology theory. Specifically, people are happiest when they are in a state of flow—a state of concentration or complete absorption with the activity at hand and the situation. It is a state in which people are so involved in an activity that nothing else seems to matter. The idea of flow is identical to the feeling of being in the zone or in the groove, what Vygotsky (1978) called the zone of proximal development.

What do Csikszentmihalyi's (1990) ideas have to do with education and our subject here? There are a couple of important ideas to understand about ZPD in order to truly appreciate its connection with student choice. First, ZPD is a "sweet spot" of sorts. Because it is a place where a student learns best, purposeful use of the sweet spot enhances the likelihood of deep learning . There is another powerful connection between ZPD and choice. In this zone, learning is most enjoyable. Whether it is a school assignment, crossword puzzle, video game, math puzzle, or science exploration, the right amount of challenge motivating.

With these understandings as a backdrop, we propose that these three theories can be considered one formula for student success. If choice can get students into a state of flow and their ZPD, you can increase their intrinsic motivation. Likewise, if—through choice—you can increase students' motivation and self-determination, you may be able to increase students' time on task, the overall quality of their work, and, hopefully, their long-term learning and feelings of accomplishment, efficacy, and agency.

Empirical Research on Choice and Motivation

Patall et al. (2010) examined the effects of providing choices among homework assignments on motivation and subsequent academic performance. In this experimental research, the authors found that when students were given choice, they reported higher intrinsic motivation to do homework, felt more competent regarding the homework, and performed better on subsequent unit tests compared to when they did not have a choice.

Patall et al. (2008) reviewed 41 studies that examined the effect of choice in a variety of settings with both children and adults. Results indicated that providing choice enhanced intrinsic motivation, effort, task performance, and perceived competence. The effect of choice was stronger in children compared to adults.

Researchers Iyengar and Lepper (2000) gave two groups of college students a weekend assignment to write a two-page essay for extra credit. The first group was given the choice of six possible essay topics; the second was given 30 choices. The counterintuitive result of the experiment? The students who were given fewer choices were more likely to turn in the assignment, and they also wrote better essays. Based upon these findings, we believe it is best to offer limited choices, especially to less experienced students who may not have had to make these decisions before. The transition to more choices should be gradual for these young people.

APPENDIX C

Interest Surveys

MY INTERESTS SURVEY ▬▬▬▬▬
(Grades K–4)

Directions: This survey will help you find topics that interest you. We will use your favorite topics to design a project you want to do. Read or listen to the names of the topics in each row.

1. Check the box next to any topic that you like so much that you would do a project about it.
2. Count the number of check marks in each row. Write that number in the last column.
3. Find the two rows that have the highest numbers.
4. Write the names of these rows on the last page.
5. Write the names of your two favorite topics on the last page, too.

	Subject	Topics	My Choices	Total From Box 1
BOX 1	**Plants, Food, and Resources**	Farms	❑	
		Growing plants	❑	
		Rain forest	❑	
		Pollution	❑	
		Fish	❑	
		Rocks, minerals, and gems	❑	
		Oceans	❑	
		Forests	❑	
		Food	❑	
		Oil and gas	❑	

MY INTERESTS SURVEY, CONTINUED

	Subject	Topics	My Choices	Total From Box 2
BOX 2	**Architecture and Buildings**	Blueprints	☐	
		Home design	☐	
		Room design	☐	
		Homes of the future	☐	
		Smart homes	☐	
		Tiny homes	☐	
		Classroom design	☐	
		School design	☐	
		Cafeteria design	☐	
		Building models	☐	

	Subject	Topics	My Choices	Total From Box 3
BOX 3	**Art, Video, Music, Technology, and Print**	Movies and YouTube	☐	
		Awards	☐	
		Newspaper reporting	☐	
		Cartoons and comics	☐	
		Dance	☐	
		Stories and poems	☐	
		Music and bands	☐	
		Drawing	☐	
		Crafts	☐	
		Songs and singing	☐	

	Subject	Topics	My Choices	Total From Box 4
BOX 4	**Businesses and Bosses**	Design a business	☐	
		Business leaders	☐	
		Report on products	☐	
		Test a product	☐	
		Create a business plan	☐	
		Design a service	☐	
		Advertise	☐	
		Find a need	☐	
		Design a product	☐	
		Customers	☐	

MY INTERESTS SURVEY, CONTINUED

	Subject	Topics	My Choices	Total From Box 5
BOX 5	**Teaching in Schools and Other Places**	Teach and coach	☐	
		Plan a lesson	☐	
		Learning activities	☐	
		Make learning fun	☐	
		Help students	☐	
		Playground problems	☐	
		Tutoring	☐	
		Study buddies	☐	
		Computer learning	☐	
		Student problems	☐	

	Subject	Topics	My Choices	Total From Box 6
BOX 6	**Budgets, Banks, and Money**	Allowances	☐	
		Savings accounts	☐	
		Stock market	☐	
		Banks	☐	
		Budgets	☐	
		Wages and salaries	☐	
		Economics	☐	
		Money and coins	☐	
		Credit cards	☐	
		Foreign money	☐	

	Subjects	Topics	My Choices	Total From Box 7
BOX 7	**Government**	Rules	☐	
		Bill of Rights	☐	
		Laws	☐	
		Civil rights	☐	
		Voting	☐	
		Elections	☐	
		Presidents	☐	
		Protests	☐	
		Leaders	☐	
		Courts	☐	

The Interest-Based Learning Coach © Prufrock Press Inc.

MY INTERESTS SURVEY, CONTINUED

	Subjects	Topics	My Choices	Total From Box 8
BOX 8	**Health and Wellness**	Exercise	☐	
		Healthy foods	☐	
		Fitness	☐	
		Illness and diseases	☐	
		Emotional health	☐	
		Drugs and alcohol	☐	
		Healthy recipes	☐	
		Mindfulness	☐	
		Nutrition	☐	
		Hunger	☐	

	Subject	Topics	My Choices	Total From Box 9
BOX 9	**Travel**	Camping and hiking	☐	
		Road trips	☐	
		Famous places	☐	
		Other countries	☐	
		U.S. travel	☐	
		Travel in my state	☐	
		Amusement parks	☐	
		National parks	☐	
		Planning trips	☐	
		Travel guides	☐	

	Subject	Topics	My Choices	Total From Box 10
BOX 10	**Helping People**	First aid	☐	
		Food banks	☐	
		Disaster help	☐	
		Hunger	☐	
		Volunteering	☐	
		Emergencies	☐	
		Charities	☐	
		Foster families	☐	
		Bullying	☐	
		Making friends	☐	

MY INTERESTS SURVEY, CONTINUED

	Subject	Topics	My Choices	Total From Box 11
BOX 11	**Computers and Technology**	Coding	☐	
		Web design	☐	
		Wikipedia	☐	
		Computer safety	☐	
		Cyberbullies	☐	
		Computers	☐	
		Drones	☐	
		Twitter and Instagram	☐	
		Texting	☐	
		Blogs	☐	

	Subject	Topics	My Choices	Total From Box 12
BOX 12	**Law, Safety, and Security**	Laws and lawyers	☐	
		Security	☐	
		Judges and courts	☐	
		Police	☐	
		Safety	☐	
		Military	☐	
		Prisons and jails	☐	
		Civil rights	☐	
		Crimes	☐	
		Rehabilitation	☐	

	Subject	Topics	My Choices	Total From Box 13
BOX 13	**Buying and Selling**	Selling	☐	
		Buying	☐	
		Advertisement	☐	
		Packaging	☐	
		Products	☐	
		Prices	☐	
		Services	☐	
		Labeling	☐	
		Finding money	☐	
		Stock market	☐	

MY INTERESTS SURVEY, CONTINUED

	Subject	Topics	My Choices	Total From Box 14
BOX 14	**Designing and Making Products**	Game design	☐	
		App design	☐	
		Toy design	☐	
		Robots	☐	
		3-D printers	☐	
		Car design	☐	
		Inventions	☐	
		Clothes design	☐	
		Jewelry design	☐	
		Card design	☐	

	Subject	Topics	My Choices	Total From Box 15
BOX 15	**Science and Math**	Animals and birds	☐	
		Weather	☐	
		Stars and planets	☐	
		Rocks	☐	
		Plants	☐	
		Oceans	☐	
		Reptiles and insects	☐	
		Chemistry	☐	
		Math games	☐	
		Math problems	☐	

	Subject	Topics	My Choices	Total From Box 16
BOX 16	**Moving People and Things**	Bikes	☐	
		Scooters, ATVs	☐	
		Cars	☐	
		Planes	☐	
		Trains	☐	
		Trucks	☐	
		Ships	☐	
		Bike paths	☐	
		Roads	☐	
		Future plans	☐	

MY INTERESTS SURVEY, CONTINUED

	Subject	Topics	My Choices	Total From Box 17
BOX 17	**Social Sciences**	Careers	❑	
		Museums	❑	
		Famous people	❑	
		College and high school	❑	
		History	❑	
		Maps	❑	
		Geography	❑	
		Cultures	❑	
		Historical places	❑	
		Social problems	❑	

	Subject	Topics	My Choices	Total From Box 18
BOX 18	**Sports, Games, and Recreation**	Sports	❑	
		Games	❑	
		Teams	❑	
		Pets	❑	
		Chess	❑	
		Coaching	❑	
		Recreation	❑	
		Announcing	❑	
		Writing	❑	
		Statistics	❑	
		Bikes, scooters, skateboards	❑	

My top two subjects/careers:

#1: _____

#2: _____

My favorite topics:

#1: _____

#2: _____

MY INTERESTS SURVEY
(Grades 5–8)

Directions: This survey will help you find topics that interest you. We will use your favorite topics to design a project you want to do. Read or listen to the names of the topics in each row.

1. Check the box next to any topic that you like so much that you would do a project about it.
2. Count the number of check marks in each row. Write that number in the last column.
3. Find the two rows that have the highest numbers.
4. Write the names of these rows on the last page.
5. Write the names of your two favorite topics on the last page, too.

	Subject	Topics	My Choices	Total From Box 1
BOX 1	**Farming, Food, and Resources**	Farms and farming	❑	
		Climate change	❑	
		Forests	❑	
		Droughts	❑	
		Rain forest	❑	
		Hunger	❑	
		Nutrition	❑	
		Nonrenewable resources	❑	
		Minerals and gems	❑	
		Oceans	❑	

MY INTERESTS SURVEY, CONTINUED

	Subject	Topics	My Choices	Total From Box 2
BOX 2	Architecture and Buildings	Factories	❑	
		Homes of the future	❑	
		Blueprints	❑	
		Smart homes	❑	
		Tiny homes	❑	
		Building supplies	❑	
		Carpentry	❑	
		Building regulations	❑	
		School/cafeteria design	❑	
		My room design	❑	

	Subject	Topics	My Choices	Total From Box 3
BOX 3	Art, Media, Music, Technology, and Communication	Films	❑	
		Film awards	❑	
		Newspaper reporting	❑	
		Authors	❑	
		Children's books	❑	
		Music	❑	
		Painting	❑	
		Ceramics	❑	
		Rap	❑	
		Cartooning/comics	❑	

	Subject	Topics	My Choices	Total From Box 4
BOX 4	Business and Bosses	Business	❑	
		Business leaders	❑	
		Design your own business	❑	
		eBay	❑	
		Product testing and reporting	❑	
		Pitch a business plan	❑	
		Design a service	❑	
		Advertising techniques	❑	
		Finding a product gap	❑	
		GoFundMe	❑	

MY INTERESTS SURVEY, CONTINUED

	Subject	Topics	My Choices	Total from Box 5
BOX 5	**Teaching in School and Business**	Lesson plans	☐	
		Making school interesting	☐	
		Autism	☐	
		Graduation requirements	☐	
		Textbooks	☐	
		Computers and hacking	☐	
		School calendars	☐	
		School hours	☐	
		Tutoring	☐	
		Learning disabilities	☐	

	Subject	Topics	My Choices	Total From Box 6
BOX 6	**Budgets, Banks, and Money**	Loans	☐	
		Banks	☐	
		Stock market	☐	
		Setting up a bank account	☐	
		Microfinancing	☐	
		Global economy	☐	
		Asking for a raise	☐	
		Interest rate	☐	
		Phone service plans	☐	
		Pay gap	☐	

	Subject	Topics	My Choices	Total From Box 7
BOX 7	**Government**	Bill of Rights	☐	
		Black Lives Matter	☐	
		Constitution	☐	
		Nuclear arms	☐	
		Political cartoons	☐	
		Presidents	☐	
		Protests	☐	
		World leaders	☐	
		Supreme Court decisions	☐	
		School law	☐	

MY INTERESTS SURVEY, CONTINUED

	Subject	Topics	My Choices	Total From Box 8
BOX 8	**Health and Wellness**	Drug and alcohol addiction	☐	
		Organic foods	☐	
		Food deserts	☐	
		Fitness	☐	
		Mental health	☐	
		Vaccinations	☐	
		Diseases	☐	
		Hospitals	☐	
		Mindfulness/yoga	☐	
		Healthy recipes	☐	

	Subject	Topics	My Choices	Total From Box 9
BOX 9	**Tourism**	Camping	☐	
		Road trips	☐	
		Sightseeing	☐	
		Hotels	☐	
		Tourists	☐	
		Cruises	☐	
		Amusement parks	☐	
		National parks	☐	
		Recreation	☐	
		Local attractions	☐	

	Subject	Topics	My Choices	Total From Box 10
BOX 10	**Helping Services and People**	Child advocacy	☐	
		Disaster relief	☐	
		Public health	☐	
		Drug abuse support	☐	
		First aid	☐	
		Lifeguarding	☐	
		School guidance counselors	☐	
		Doctors	☐	
		Nurses	☐	
		Clergy	☐	

MY INTERESTS SURVEY, CONTINUED

	Subject	Topics	My Choices	Total From Box 11
BOX 11	**Computer Technology**	Hacking	☐	
		Web design	☐	
		Coding	☐	
		Instagram	☐	
		Texting	☐	
		Drones	☐	
		Cyber security	☐	
		Impact of technology	☐	
		Twitter	☐	
		iPhones	☐	

	Subject	Topics	My Choices	Total From Box 12
BOX 12	**Law, Safety, and Security**	Cyberbullying	☐	
		Civil rights	☐	
		Gun violence	☐	
		Immigration/migration	☐	
		Social movements	☐	
		Supreme Court	☐	
		Judges	☐	
		Lawyers	☐	
		Police	☐	
		Military	☐	

	Subject	Topics	My Choices	Total From Box 13
BOX 13	**Buying and Selling**	Advertising	☐	
		Advertisements	☐	
		Marketing strategies	☐	
		Telemarketing	☐	
		Packaging	☐	
		Shopping	☐	
		Illegal data gathering	☐	
		Website design	☐	
		Pricing	☐	
		Market competition	☐	

MY INTERESTS SURVEY, CONTINUED

	Subject	Topics	My Choices	Total From Box 14
BOX 14	**Factories and Designing and Making Products**	Design engineering	❑	
		Safety	❑	
		Artificial intelligence	❑	
		Tools and equipment	❑	
		Robots	❑	
		3-D printers	❑	
		Apprenticeships	❑	
		Manufacturing skills gap	❑	
		Car design	❑	
		Imports/exports	❑	

	Subject	Topics	My Choices	Total From Box 15
BOX 15	**Science, Technology, Engineering, and Mathematics (STEM)**	Animals	❑	
		Birds	❑	
		Black holes	❑	
		Cloning	❑	
		Coral bleaching	❑	
		E-cigarettes	❑	
		Surveys/questionnaires	❑	
		Cartography	❑	
		Statistics	❑	
		Earth/life/physical sciences	❑	

	Subject	Topics	My Choices	Total From Box 16
BOX 16	**Moving People and Things Now and in the Future**	Electric cars	❑	
		Transporting goods	❑	
		Fast trains	❑	
		Bike paths	❑	
		Solar roadways	❑	
		Transportation emissions	❑	
		Drone technology	❑	
		Amazon Prime	❑	
		Road and bridge repair	❑	
		Trucking	❑	

Name: _____ Date: _____

MY INTERESTS SURVEY, CONTINUED

	Subject	Topics	My Choices	Total From Box 17
BOX 17	**Fashion**	Body image	☐	
		Clothes	☐	
		Pattern making	☐	
		Sewing	☐	
		Fashion design	☐	
		Makeup	☐	
		Textiles	☐	
		Men's fashion	☐	
		Fashion designers	☐	
		Models	☐	

	Subject	Topics	My Choices	Total From Box 18
BOX 18	**Sports, Games and Recreation**	Basketball	☐	
		Football	☐	
		Soccer	☐	
		Sports teams	☐	
		Rules of sport games	☐	
		Chess	☐	
		Recreation	☐	
		Television sports	☐	
		Gymnastics	☐	
		Skiing	☐	

My top two subjects/careers:

#1: _____

#2: _____

My favorite topics:

#1: _____

#2: _____

APPENDIX D
Product Finder

PRODUCT FINDER

Directions: This listing of real-world products by career cluster might help you identify possible products for your IBL project. Do any of these appeal to you and align with your project? Check those that you especially like. When you have selected possible products from the different clusters, select your top two favorites and write them on the spaces provided at the end.

	Career Cluster	Products	My Choices
BOX 1	**Farming, Food, and Resources**	Maps	❑
		Research reports	❑
		Newspaper story	❑
		Public awareness campaign	❑
		Radio/TV infomercial	❑
		Instruction booklet	❑
		Pamphlet	❑
		Database	❑
		Letters to local/state officials	❑
		PowerPoint or Prezi presentation	❑

	Career Cluster	Products	My Choices
BOX 2	**Architecture and Buildings**	Blueprint	❑
		Building design	❑
		Room design	❑
		Informational pamphlet	❑
		Transcribed interviews	❑
		Photo essay	❑
		Poster	❑
		Urban renewal plan	❑
		PointPoint or Prezi	❑
		Public awareness campaign	❑

PRODUCT FINDER, CONTINUED

Career Cluster	Products	My Choices
BOX 3 **Art, Media, Music, Technology, and Communication**	Book	☐
	Book talk	☐
	Interview	☐
	Dramatic reading	☐
	Movie review	☐
	Museum exhibit	☐
	Newspaper article	☐
	Exhibit of original art	☐
	Musical performance	☐
	iMovie	☐

Career Cluster	Products	My Choices
BOX 4 **Business and Bosses**	Press conference	☐
	Interview with business leader(s)	☐
	Business plan	☐
	Product testing report	☐
	GoFundMe campaign	☐
	Fundraising campaign	☐
	Survey with results	☐
	Data analysis	☐
	Editorial	☐
	Trend predictions	☐

Career Cluster	Products	My Choices
BOX 5 **Teaching in School and Business**	Lesson plans	☐
	Informational pamphlet	☐
	Debate: School calendars	☐
	Making school interesting plan	☐
	Tutoring plan	☐
	Interviews with students, teachers, administrators	☐
	PowerPoint or Prezi: School hacking	☐
	Reviews of movies featuring educators/ education	☐

PRODUCT FINDER, CONTINUED

	Career Cluster	Products	My Choices
BOX 6	**Budgets, Banks, and Money**	Press conference	❏
		Charts/illustrations	❏
		Fundraising campaign	❏
		Infomercial	❏
		Presentation	❏
		Trend analysis	❏
		Start-up business	❏
		Petition	❏
		Editorial	❏
		Invention	❏

	Career Cluster	Products	My Choices
BOX 7	**Government**	Social action campaign	❏
		Political action campaign	❏
		Foreign policy analysis	❏
		Political cartoon museum	❏
		Campaign for school/local office	❏
		Podcast	❏
		YouTube video	❏
		Oral history	❏
		Debate	❏
		Panel discussion	❏

	Career Cluster	Products	My Choices
BOX 8	**Health and Wellness**	YouTube video	❏
		Fitness plan	❏
		Charts and graphs	❏
		Investigative report	❏
		Service program	❏
		Magazine or newspaper story	❏
		Advertisement/public service announcement	❏
		Demonstration	❏
		Podcast	❏

PRODUCT FINDER, CONTINUED

	Career Cluster	Products	My Choices
BOX 9	**Tourism**	Travel brochure	☐
		Webpage	☐
		Slideshow	☐
		Map	☐
		MapQuest	☐
		Documentary	☐
		YouTube video	☐
		Travel advice website	☐
		Debate: medical tourism	☐
		Audiotape	☐

	Career Cluster	Products	My Choices
BOX 10	**Helping Services and People**	An app	☐
		Computer game	☐
		Public awareness campaign: Disinformation	☐
		Charts/graphs	☐
		Resource map	☐
		Pamphlet	☐
		Podcast	☐
		Radio program	☐
		Editorial	☐
		Poster	☐

	Career Cluster	Products	My Choices
BOX 11	**Computer Technology**	Webpage	☐
		Pamphlet	☐
		TV or radio segment	☐
		Debate: security of the Internet	☐
		YouTube video	☐
		Editorial	☐
		Trend analysis	☐
		Social media marketing plan	☐
		Promotional brochure	☐

PRODUCT FINDER, CONTINUED

Career Cluster	Products	My Choices
BOX 12 **Law, Safety, and Security**	Charts/graphs	❑
	Debate: Guns in school	❑
	Documentary	❑
	Interviews	❑
	Investigative report	❑
	Mural/timeline of civil rights	❑
	Oral history	❑
	Presentation	❑
	Publication	❑
	Social action campaign	❑

Career Cluster	Products	My Choices
BOX 13 **Buying and Selling**	Environmental campaign	❑
	Robotics program	❑
	Awareness pamphlet	❑
	TED Talk	❑
	Background research on a manufacturing problem	❑
	Model	❑
	Timeline	❑
	Feasibility study	❑
	Panel discussion: Future manufacturing	❑
	Skills gap	❑

Career Cluster	Products	My Choices
BOX 14 **Factories and Designing and Making Products**	Design of an object	❑
	Packaging design	❑
	Awareness pamphlet	❑
	Feasibility study	❑
	Model(s) with field trials	❑
	Public awareness campaign	❑
	Repair manual	❑
	YouTube video	❑
	Whiteboard animated video	❑
	TED Talk	❑

Name: _____ Date: _____

PRODUCT FINDER, CONTINUED

	Career Cluster	Products	My Choices
BOX 15	**Science, Technology, Engineering, and Mathematics (STEM)**	Artifact collection	❏
		Windmill design	❏
		Field study	❏
		Invention	❏
		Research study	❏
		Maps	❏
		Sustainability study	❏
		Interviews	❏
		Debates	❏
		TED Talk	❏

	Career Cluster	Products	My Choices
BOX 16	**Moving People and Things Now and in the Future**	Maps	❏
		Photo essay	❏
		Radio program	❏
		Museum exhibit	❏
		Advertisement	❏
		Editorial	❏
		Children's book: Drone technology	❏
		Model	❏
		Survey	❏
		TED Talk	❏

	Career Cluster	Products	My Choices
BOX 17	**Fashion**	Body image presentation	❏
		Pattern(s)	❏
		Original clothes	❏
		Market research on makeup	❏
		Charts/graphs	❏
		Awareness pamphlet	❏
		Timeline of designers	❏
		Photo essay	❏
		TED Talk: Sustainable fashion designs	❏

PRODUCT FINDER, CONTINUED

	Career Cluster	Products	My Choices
BOX 18	**Sports, Games, and Recreation**	Charts/graphs	❑
		Playbook	❑
		Town webpage	❑
		Surveys	❑
		Playground design	❑
		Interviews	❑
		Awareness pamphlet	❑
		Rule booklet	❑
		Summer recreation plan	❑

My top two favorite product formats that are aligned with my project:

1. _____

2. _____

ABOUT THE AUTHORS

Jeanne H. Purcell, Ph.D., completed her B.A. at the University of Hartford in British literature, and 2 years later she finished a master's degree in urban education. In 1993 she completed a Ph.D. in educational psychology at the University of Connecticut. Jeanne began teaching in 1973 at the secondary level in Hartford, CT. Over her career of 40 years, she taught in urban, rural, and suburban districts. She completed her formal career in 2009 at the Connecticut State Department of Education, where, for a decade, she provided leadership for gifted and talented education initiatives. Jeanne has fond memories of art classes and teachers who allowed students to study and complete a landscape of choice, along with a similar opportunity to study and complete a still life of choice. Jeanne recalls that, at the time, these opportunities seemed so liberating. She learned early about the power of choice and the opportunity to direct her own learning. And from that time forward, she deeply appreciated any choices that were afforded her in a formal schooling situation.

Deborah E. Burns, Ph.D., earned her B.S. from Michigan State University, her M.S. degree from Ashland (OH) University, and her Ph.D. from the University of Connecticut. In September 2018, Deb celebrated 45 years of delightful and diverse experiences within the education community. She began her career working with K–8 students in a Marshall, MI, Title I remedial reading and math program. She went on to serve as a K–4 classroom teacher, a middle school language arts and gifted education teacher, a regional gifted education specialist, a professor, a district curriculum director, and a consultant for the Association for Supervision and

Curriculum Development. Deb's first memory of an interest-based learning experience was with her fifth-grade teacher in Dearborn, MI. Noticing some of her students' enthusiasm for both plays and U.S. pioneer history, Ms. Ivadelle Moore coaxed, mentored, and made time for their playwriting, costuming, set design, and production efforts! Bravo, Ms. Moore!

Wellesley H. Purcell completed his B.A. in English at Eastern Connecticut State University and his M.A. in education at Sacred Heart University. During the summer months, he completed Advanced Placement seminars conducted jointly by the College Board and Eastern Connecticut State University. Welles began teaching in the Hartford, CT, elementary schools as a literacy interventionist and as a kindergarten teacher. He has also taught English and language arts classes at the middle school and high school levels in both Maine and Connecticut. His first recollection of interest-based learning was in eighth grade when his social studies teacher offered his class the opportunity to put together a World War II museum with artifacts and oral histories from students' family members. The entire community was invited to attend the museum. The project was a touchstone moment for Welles, and it has influenced the way he teaches his students. He recognizes the power of interest-based learning because of its unique motivational power, and he regularly uses the instructional strategy in his own classrooms.